HOW TO WIN
ARGUMENTS

DEDICATED TO

all those allies and adversaries,
at college and law school,
at Shearman & Sterling
and *National Review,*
on radio and television,
who have instructed me
in the fine art of
winning arguments

"In my youth," said his father, "I took to the law,
And argued each case with my wife;
And the muscular strength, which it gave to my jaw,
Has lasted the rest of my life."

Alice in Wonderland
Lewis Carroll

HOW TO WIN ARGUMENTS

William A. Rusher

UNIVERSITY
PRESS OF
AMERICA

Copyright © 1981 by

William A. Rusher

University Press of America,® Inc.

4720 Boston Way
Lanham, MD 20706

Printed in the United States of America

This edition published in 1985 by
University Press of America, Inc., by
arrangement with Doubleday & Company, Inc.

Library of Congress Cataloging in Publication Data

Rusher, William A., 1923-
  How to win arguments.
  Reprint. Originally published: Garden City, N. Y. :
Doubleday, c 1981.
Includes index.
  1. Debates and debating. I. Title.
PN4181.R8   1985   808'.53   85-13344
ISBN 0-8191-4771-0   (pbk. : alk. paper)

All University Press of America books are produced on acid-free
paper which exceeds the minimum standards set by the National
Historical Publications and Records Commission.

FOREWORD

This book is an attempt to put between covers, informally and with appropriate illustrations, most of what the author has learned about argumentation in the course of a lifetime devoted to arguing: personally, professionally, and politically.

It is not, therefore, a formal tract on logic, or a rigorous scientific survey of the principles of rhetoric, replete with Latin terms for each type of fallacy. Such taxonomic hornbooks have their uses; but this volume is intended to enlighten and entertain the average American, and he or she will rarely feel comfortable—or even be effective— pointing out to a spouse, or employer, or opposing debater that the latter has just been guilty of (say) an *ignoratio elenchi*.

My qualifications for writing this book are to be found in my life history, and they are so comprehensive that they occasionally startle even me. In early 1937, at the age of 13, I joined and was soon running my high school debating club, aptly called the Filibusters. At Princeton, in 1940–42, I won the Hope Freshman Prize Debate and then became a member, and finally manager, of the Varsity Debate Team. After the war I enrolled in Harvard Law School, and on graduation spent seven and a half years in the litigation department of Shearman & Sterling—then as now Wall Street's largest law firm. Next came seventeen months as special counsel to the Internal Security Subcommittee of the United States Senate. The remaining twenty-four years of my life to date have been spent as publisher of *National Review*, America's leading journal of conservative opinion.

In the latter capacity I have had numerous occasions to engage in intramural arguments with such redoubtable gladiators as William F. Buckley, Jr., James Burnham, and the late Frank S. Meyer. In addition, as a spokesman for the conservative movement, I have argued for that cause in just about every public forum available in the American society: before college and business audiences (in debates and otherwise), on radio and television talk shows of every imaginable description, and against a vast and formidable array of adversaries. From 1970 to 1973 I was the regular conservative advocate on the Emmy-winning PBS television program, "The Advocates"; from 1976 to 1979 I was under contract to ABC Television to appear regularly in the "Face Off" debates featured on "Good Morning, America." It would be odd indeed if I had undergone that sort of lifelong ordeal by oratorical fire without learning a fair amount about the black arts of argumentation. Herein is what I learned.

Throughout I have tried to use specific illustrations for my points, whenever memory or other sources made them available. Since my "Advocates" programs were transcribed and I have a complete set of the transcripts, I have been able to draw on that source especially heavily—thereby giving rise to what may prove, to some readers, a problem. So many of my public arguments have been on behalf of the conservative cause that passionate liberals may feel their side is not fully or fairly treated in the illustrations I have necessarily chosen. Wherever possible, therefore, I have tried to balance illustrations drawn from my own debates with others that liberal readers will enjoy more—e.g., the account of Richard Nixon's sly but unsuccessful joust with Bill Buckley in 1958. In general, however, I hope that the unavoidable bias in my selection of examples can be overlooked, and that the book will prove entertaining and helpful to people of all political viewpoints and none.

I cannot close without recording my gratitude to Claire Wirth, who not only transcribed the entire manuscript from my minuscule and clumsy handwriting but provided by her own example a continuing reminder of how far it is possible for sheer graciousness to supplant, in human affairs, the law of the jungle; to Dorothy McCartney, who meticulously checked and corrected numerous factual assertions; and, last but far from least, to Bill Adler, who taught me, on our very first joint enterprise, just how good a friend, how valuable an adviser, and how indispensable a representative a really first-class book agent can be.

William A. Rusher

CONTENTS

I

WHY ARGUE?

Many people, perhaps most, would be happy if they never had to argue at all. Certainly many will go to almost any length to avoid an argument if they possibly can.

Partly, no doubt, this is due to something very like fear. Arguing, after all, almost by definition involves *disagreeing,* and some people simply cannot bring themselves to offer another person what they conceive to be the *affront* of disagreeing with him.

Then again, a distaste for arguing may be based simply on the conviction—often derived from experience—that one is likely to lose. In such cases there may be no aversion to arguing *per se:* quite the contrary! But in an argument the outcome depends in part on the skill of the protagonists, and a person keenly aware of his lack of skill may, like a general with a poorly trained army, prefer retreat to defeat.

Finally, opposition to the idea of arguing may be purely philosophical, or, if you prefer, temperamental. There is a sort of serene personality for whom arguing is simply not worth the trouble. The British author Walter Savage Landor expressed this above-it-all attitude engagingly in the first line of a famous quatrain:

> *I strove with none, for none was worth my strife;*
> *Nature I love; and next to nature, art.*
> *I warmed both hands before the fire of life;*
> *It sinks, and I am ready to depart.*

Whether the disinclination to argue is psychological, practical, or philosophical, however, there undoubtedly do come times when we are all forced to argue. The pathologically shy person finds himself compelled to defend one position and thus (at least by implication) attack another. The untrained and inadequate disputant is obliged, ready or not, to dispute. No doubt even Landor found it necessary, now and then, to "strive with" someone, however unworthy that someone may have been of Landor's strife.

This is, in other words, a crowded and disputatious world, and there is simply no getting through it without crossing swords with others from time to time—verbally, if we are lucky; literally, if we are not.

The latter point, incidentally, puts arguing in a somewhat better light than Landor's disdain for it implies. Wild animals and primitive men don't argue: They simply square off and fight. Arguing— defined as the stating of a case for or against something—presupposes a certain minimum amount of communication and even orderly discussion. It is, in short, a civilized substitute for far blunter means of resolving disputes.

As a practical matter in any case, the occasions for arguments abound on every side, and they can rarely be avoided altogether for so much as a single day.

Mr. X gets up in the morning and promptly encounters that whole continent of opportunities for disagreement (and therefore arguments) represented by domestic life. Even the most affectionate married couple will have disagreements on a host of subjects; the fact is not even regarded, in most civilized jurisdictions, as a ground for divorce. (Asked whether she had ever contemplated a divorce from Alfred Lunt, Lynn Fontanne replied, "No. Murder, many times; divorce, never.")

If Mr. X's wife is exceptionally tractable this morning, there are still the children. Does any parent need to be reminded how often life with a teenager can resemble playing host to a visiting debate team?

Then there are the in-laws—a clan so pestiferous that our folk-memory reserves an entire category of jokes to cope with them. Archie Bunker isn't by a long shot the only father-in-law whose life is a running battle with his daughter's husband.

If Mr. X manages to make it out the front door reasonably intact, he can look forward to another score of occasions for arguments lying in wait for him at the office.

Even if his work environment is one of the rare ones in which arguments with people above and below one's level in the hierarchy never occur because all decisions are made according to rank, he must still contend with his equals. And, depending on the nature of his business, his workday will also involve, to a greater or lesser extent, all sorts of encounters with outside individuals and organizations with whom the business must deal—each encounter carrying its own potential for disagreement.

In addition to sustaining the abrasions necessarily involved in his job, Mr. X—and for that matter Mrs. X—must cope every day with a whole series of service personnel of one sort or another: postmen, telephone repairmen, waiters, cabdrivers, etc., some of them with chips situated very loosely on their shoulders. (I pause here to nominate, as by long odds the most argumentative bunch I have ever encountered, New York City's cabdrivers. Winning an argument with one of these can therefore be an exhilarating experience indeed, but the attempt should only be made by persons possessing an intimate knowledge of New York geography, a law degree, a pair of leather lungs, and a mean streak.)

Another whole category of almost inevitable disagreements revolves around our necessary encounters with Authority in one form or another: traffic cops, City Hall, Internal Revenue agents, etc. In spite of the old dictum that "You can't fight City Hall," there are times when we must. There are even times when one can win such an argument. The basic techniques for arguing with the various echelons of government are a highly specialized subdivision of the general art of argumentation, however, and will accordingly be dealt with in a section all their own.

Finally, to most of us there will sooner or later come a time when we are asked to engage in some more formal type of argumentation: a panel discussion at the local PTA, a radio or TV talk show, a business "presentation," etc. At a minimum, most parents will someday have to advise their bairn on how to win, or at least participate respectably in, some high school debate. Such discussions are governed by more or less formal rules, and knowing the rules—and how to benefit from them—is the essential first step toward intelligent participation.

There is, then, no practical way to avoid engaging in arguments to a certain extent. One need not (indeed, ought not to) seek out opportunities to argue; they will find us, never fear. But when one does —when an argument becomes unavoidable—it will behoove us to know a few practical rules about how to win, or at least battle to a draw. That is what this book is all about.

It is not a correspondence course in formal logic, or even a handbook on the formal science of argumentation, carefully distinguishing the Argument from Definition and the Argument from Circumstance, or specifying precisely when to use the deadly *reductio ad absurdum*. Such works have their place, but they are not the book America badly needs and that this seeks to be: a useful guide for laymen through the thickets of daily argumentation.

Before proceeding directly to cases, however, it is important to clear away some preliminary underbrush: possible alternatives to arguing; the purpose of arguing; and the arguer as a type.

II

ALTERNATIVES TO ARGUING

Perhaps the commonest alternative to arguing is negotiation and compromise. These are not, however, polar alternatives to arguing: Almost every negotiation leading to compromise is preceded and/or accompanied by that "statement of a case for or against something" which is the very definition of argumentation. Many an argument slowly resolves, as the issues become defined and the parties' respective positions are stated, into a search for common ground on which a compromise can be based. Conversely, more than one negotiation which everyone had hoped would result in a compromise has resulted instead in a hardening of positions in which all that is possible is the sort of argumentation that "clarifies the issues."

If the matter at stake is important enough to us, we will often decide to turn the conduct of the whole controversy over to a professional arguer: i.e., a lawyer. For that, after all, is what a lawyer fundamentally is: a person hired to argue somebody else's case. In the English courts of the Middle Ages a person with a complaint (or someone who had been complained against) originally pleaded his own case. Gradually, however, inarticulate or ignorant litigants fell into the habit of seeking the help of professional pleaders who hung around the courts, thereby becoming familiar with the procedures, the judges, the writs available to remedy particular wrongs, etc. Inevitably, as the number and complexity of lawsuits grew, the whole process tended to become increasingly bureaucratized. The professional pleader became not merely a convenience, but a downright necessity to his client and, scarcely less, to the judge. At last the judges would consent to hear only persons previously "admitted to the bar" of the court—and lawyers had established their monopoly.

A modern lawyer, then, is primarily and supremely a professional arguer. He will listen to his client's case and quickly identify its chief points—and its weaknesses, if any. He will usually have a far better idea than the client of how best to proceed: by negotiation, by a lawsuit, or by still other means. Standing a bit to one side of the controversy, he will ordinarily be able to bring valuable objectivity to bear on it. Countless are the clients who have benefited from the wise advice of experienced lawyers—though, of course, lawyers are fallible, too, in all the ways known to our fallen race.

The beauty of putting a serious argument in the hands of a competent lawyer is that one is entitled thereafter to feel reasonably confident that the argument will be well conducted. In all likelihood the level of acrimony will drop to near zero. Whether a lawsuit is filed or not, the client's case will be analyzed carefully and stated as well as the surrounding circumstances permit. Ordinarily, the other protagonist will be tempted, or compelled, to reply on the same dryly rational level. The process will continue, if necessary under rules laid down by the courts for such situations, until the issues are well defined, and all available relevant evidence has been adduced (or is waiting in the wings), and the lawyers have made their final pleas or are ready to do so. Then, if the parties still cannot settle their argument amicably, a court will settle it for them.

Much the same things that we have said about lawyers and courts apply to all those quasi-judicial groups and individuals—arbitration boards, baseball commissioners, marriage counselors, etc.—who also specialize in refereeing other peoples' arguments. By far the most useful and generally applicable variant of the species, however, is the lawyer. He is the lubricant of society's essential machinery, making sure as far as possible that its parts mesh rather than clash. Or, to vary the metaphor, he is a sort of universal interpreter, making the words of one speaker intelligible to another: a function truly essential to any polyglot civilization.

However poetically we describe him though, the lawyer remains basically a professional arguer: a hired stater of cases. And tempted as we might be to wish that every argument could be left in his hands, there are obviously circumstances in which we ourselves must do the arguing. The disagreement may be too trivial, or for some other reason inappropriate for reference to a lawyer. There are for instance whole categories of important disputes (e.g., the "I love you darling, *but*" variety) which one or both parties would be mortally offended to see referred to a lawyer.

So lawyers, valuable as they are, do not—any more than negotiation and compromise—offer us any assured escape from the occasional iron necessity to argue.

III

THE BASIC PURPOSES
OF ARGUING

Thus far we have proceeded on the implicit assumption that the purpose of arguing is to win: to state the case for or against something so convincingly that we prevail. "Prevailing," in this context, may merely mean gaining another person or group's assent to a given proposition; or it may involve inducing some particular action.

But a moment's reflection will confirm that people often have other reasons for arguing: unacknowledged or even unconscious reasons that have little or nothing to do with "prevailing" or "winning." We ourselves are more subject to irrational impulses than we usually realize or care to admit. And even if we personally never argue for any but the most pressing and justifiable of reasons, we assuredly live in a world where plenty of other people do. In order to prevail over our adversary, it is important to understand his real reason for arguing—a reason of which he himself may be wholly unaware.

One of the commonest reasons people argue, aside from a serious need to prevail, is simply to work off their aggressions. Most of us live in an environment that, in one way or another, crowds us too closely from time to time. We are surrounded by too many people, or put under too great a time pressure, or called upon to perform at a level beyond our capacity. We are abused or treated unfairly or (sometimes worst of all) simply ignored. It is perfectly natural to react to one of those disagreeable experiences by resenting it. When the accumulated resentments reach a high enough level, we may erupt in one direction or in another: inward upon ourselves, or outward upon our family, friends, and colleagues, by picking an argument. Our accumulated resentments become displaced onto the nominal subject of the argument, which frequently turns into a shouting match. Yet afterward one or both parties may feel a great deal better: The argument cleared the air. More accurately, it cleared the bile duct.

I myself remember engaging regularly in this sort of purgative argument when I was serving at U. S. Air Force Headquarters in Calcutta in 1944–45. I was the veriest shavetail, having worn the gold bar of a second lieutenant for less than a year. The boss of my section was a major from Alabama with a bandit moustache and a general cultural level reflective, shall we say, of his background milieu. We were both oppressed by Calcutta's heat, sorry to be in India at all, and just generally overworked. And thus it became a ritual, at least for a while, that every morning punctually at nine I would walk over to his desk and we would have an argument. As the junior partner in these festivities I took care not to push the major's patience too far; but it soon became clear that he was getting as much out of these sessions as I was. I have long since forgotten what our disputes were nominally about—presumably some aspect of supply, which was the chief concern of my section—but it doesn't matter. By 9:15 we had both worked our adrenalin up to the operating level and were ready for the day.

Some people, of course, accumulate resentments more quickly than others and discharge them more easily through arguments. There are, in addition, plenty of people who are just "naturally aggressive," and employ the same technique to work off their aggressive impulses safely and conveniently. I am probably one of these, and another is Charles Morgan, the courtly Southern liberal who was for years the Washington Director of the American Civil Liberties Union.

For a time Charlie and I were both under contract to argue regularly on the "Face Off" mini-debates on ABC-TV's "Good Morning, America." One morning Charlie was arguing some point of public policy that gave him the opportunity to lash out at one of his favorite targets: business corporations, I think. Anyway, I recognized his line of argument as one that gave him quite a bonus in jollies that had little to do with the real merits of the case. Deciding to imply as much for the benefit of the audience, I tut-tutted his attack on corporations as personally motivated, and then advised him crisply to "Work out your neuroses on your own time."

It is one measure of Charlie Morgan's greatness that he didn't even bother to deny the implication. He merely chuckled and replied, as I recall, "If I did that, we'd be here all day!"

A truly tremendous number of arguments, then, from the household variety all the way up to congressional debates, are fueled much more extensively than is sometimes realized by this need to work off aggressions. There is nothing wrong with this, or at least nothing that can ordinarily be done to prevent it; but we ought to be quick to recognize it, in ourselves or others, if only because it is a waste of time to squander a lot of heavy logic on situations that are simply not designed to respond to purely logical treatment.

Another frequent reason for arguing (other than winning), and an extremely useful one, is in order to clarify an issue or problem. This differs from "clearing the air," discussed above, which involves chiefly the ventilating of emotions. However, many a knotty problem has been usefully clarified by the process of argumentation—often, though not always, to the point where it simply disappears.

This happens all the time in those most ritualized and systematic of all arguments: lawsuits. The vast majority of lawsuits never get to trial at all, and this is very largely due to the careful procedural steps that are prescribed before a trial can begin—which serve to clarify the issues. Let me describe these procedures; they are not fundamentally different from what goes on more informally in many a less stylized argument.

The plaintiff in a typical lawsuit files a "complaint," specifying what he alleges has happened and why he ought to be awarded a verdict for money damages against the defendant. The defendant files an "answer," ordinarily admitting some of the facts alleged by the plaintiff and denying others. He often also alleges further facts not mentioned by the plaintiff. This process goes on, back and forth, sometimes with the plaintiff filing one or more "amended complaints," and the defendant filing a similar series of "amended answers," until the factual issues really in dispute stand out sharply. At this point, if a judge is satisfied that the plaintiff's allegations would, *if proved*, entitle him to a judgment against the defendant, the process of "pleading" is considered complete.

Trial is still far away however. The next stage, ordinarily, is a series of "examinations before trial," in which attorneys for each side probe the case that will be offered by the other: by inspecting his records, and questioning his witnesses under oath. The purpose here is to ascertain how solid the opponent's case really is—and, collaterally, to find out just how weak or strong one's own case may be.

It is quite extraordinary how educational and sobering this process can be. A quarter of a century ago when I was an associate in the litigation department of Wall Street's largest law firm (then called Shearman & Sterling & Wright), I spent over three years as the most junior member of a three-man team defending the National City Bank of New York against a lawsuit for $2,200,000 brought by Tabacalera, a Spanish corporation with vast sugar and tobacco holdings in the Philippines. One of the absolutely essential allegations in Tabacalera's complaint against National City was that Tabacalera had had no independent legal advice concerning a certain transaction. In the course of our "examination before trial" of Tabacalera's witnesses and records, however—an examination far more extensive and intensive than Tabacalera's own attorneys had made—we came upon a cable from Tabacalera's home office in Barcelona to its local office in Manila squarely quoting the advice of lawyers in Spain concerning the transaction in question.*

The discovery and disclosure of that single cable—which was just one of over twelve hundred documents we extracted from Tabacalera in the course of a fourteen-month "examination before trial"—ended the case: Tabacalera settled the suit by paying the defendant, National City Bank, five-sixths of the latter's $600,000 counterclaim!

But arguing for the purpose of clarification—or at any rate with the consequence of clarification—isn't confined to courtrooms. As a

* I say "we came upon a cable." In fact, of course, Tabacalera and its attorneys found the cable in the company's files during a search in response to our general demand for any such communications and, being honorable men, turned it over to us when the judge ruled that it was indeed relevant. (Incidentally, it was not privileged as a communication between attorney and client because Tabacalera had "waived" the privilege by alleging in its complaint that it had received no legal advice on the transaction in question.)

matter of fact, far more disagreements in this world are based on simple factual misunderstandings than on true differences of any sort, and the former tend to evaporate swiftly when the process of arguing reveals and clarifies the misunderstanding. One of the very few sharp verbal clashes I have ever had with my colleague Bill Buckley arose as a result of such a misunderstanding.

As owner and editor of *National Review*, Buckley rightly gives his personal attention to the magazine's color covers, which, of course, have a major effect on its looks and impact in purely editorial terms. As *National Review*'s publisher I have an equally lively interest in the subject, since both circulation and advertising can be affected by the covers too.

A good many years ago a controversy arose because certain people over on the editorial side wanted something concerning the covers done in a particular way (frankly, I've forgotten how). The man who was then our advertising manager had what seemed to him equally cogent reasons for wanting it done another way. Both sides appealed their case up the chain of command, until the squabble reached Buckley and me. At that point Bill and I conferred amicably, arrived at a satisfactory compromise, and forgot about it.

A few days later the advertising manager (let's call him John Jones) told me in a fury that a certain editor (hereinafter, Jack Smith) had just informed him that the covers would, after all, be done the editorial department's way, Buckley having thus decreed that very afternoon. I promptly phoned Bill and told him in my most acid tone that, if hereafter he decided to overturn such agreements between us, I would appreciate the courtesy of at least being notified. Bill replied, drop for hydrochloric drop, that he didn't know what I was talking about and would I care to go lie down somewhere until I recovered my poise? I snapped back that, instead, I would get to the bottom of precisely who was saying what to whom. Buckley: "Please do!" We hung up simultaneously.

I summoned Jones and Smith and marched both of them straight into Buckley's office.

RUSHER to JONES: "Did you or didn't you tell me that Smith said Buckley had decided thus and so?"

JONES: "Yes. [to Smith:] Didn't you say that Buckley had decided thus and so?"

SMITH: "Yes. Well, not exactly . . ."

Ah! There it was: a slightly different version of what Buckley had actually told Smith. As Smith gave his version, Buckley interrupted to modify it still further. The three of them were clearly getting back together on the subject, and I left before the conversation was even over. Later that day Bill said to me, "I'm glad you brought Jones and Smith down here to straighten things out." So was I. Our respective colleagues, accidentally or otherwise, had very nearly embroiled Buckley and me in an ugly spat.

Of course, clarification in this case, as in most cases, was technically the argument's by-product rather than its purpose. But a great many disputes (this was a classic example) are founded so totally on a sheer misunderstanding that arguing them out is really better defined as a way of dissipating them through clarification than as a means to the end of "winning."

We shall return to this key matter of the *purpose* of arguing when we discuss the threshold questions that must be considered before entering into a serious argument. For even within the general context of a rational desire to prevail, there are various refinements of an argument's purpose that need to be distinguished: winning at once versus winning in the long run, winning as a matter of cold logic versus winning the audience, etc. Meanwhile, simply remember that—as illustrated above—there are many arguments waged for reasons that have little or nothing to do with "winning."

IV

THE ARGUER AS A TYPE

A person not fond of arguing is likely to suspect that some people have a natural proclivity for argument: They enjoy it, are good at it, frequently engage in it, and tend to "win." How true is this, and—if true—what does it imply for those who are not "natural arguers"?

I think it is best to recognize at the outset that some people do indeed have a special knack, or bent, for arguing. Arguing is, after all, simply one subdivision of the necessary human function of communicating. On the law of averages, some people will be better than others at this particular subdivision—just as other people will be better at other subdivisions: They become our orators, poets, etc. For that matter, some people will be better communicators in general— just as some will be better painters, musicians, engineers, chefs. That is no reason (as we shall see below) why a person not naturally skilled in arguing should throw in the towel when confronted with an adept. It is enough merely to note the fact that adepts exist.

What makes one person a more skillful arguer than another? The relevant attributes fall into two categories: natural and acquired.

Among the natural attributes of skilled arguers, one of the commonest and most important is an exceptionally quick mind. Many years ago Bill Buckley told me, "I don't think I have an exceptionally powerful mind, but I do think I have an exceptionally quick one." Without derogating the power of Buckley's mind, which is not to be sneezed at, I believe he was correct: His mind moves with extraordinary rapidity through the ganglia of an argument—rejecting a dozen alternative contentions to choose the best, formulating a witty statement of the chosen position, and blasting off on a fresh tack before his bewildered adversary can comprehend, let alone answer, his point.

Moreover, please note that this sort of blitz has all sorts of collateral advantages. If by any chance the position adopted was not the best, or at any rate is in fact vulnerable, Buckley may be miles away and regaling the audience with an anecdote before his opponent can launch an offensive against the position. If he insists on attacking it anyway, he will sound irrelevant at worst and plodding at best.

Related to this natural gift of speed, and yet distinct from it, is what might be called a "naturally well-ordered mind." Some people seem to have, independently of any training they may have received, minds in which there is a place for everything and everything is in its place. Such people tend to be intellectually calm and rather rigorous; they are comfortably aware of where they are, what is happening, and (in terms of argumentation) what the thread of the discussion is. They are the precise opposite of the harum-scarum, bird-brained mentality affected by comedians of the Phyllis Diller type.

The possessor of such a well-ordered mind will typically recall a wandering argument to its basic theme with some such remark as, "That's not the point," or "I thought we were discussing . . ." or "What are you saying?"—traffic signs along the road of the argument, as it were.

Among acquired (as distinguished from natural) skills in argumentation, one may note poise, clarity of thought and expression, a basic understanding of logical processes, and a willingness to state the case for a soundly considered view.

First, poise. The person who comes to an argument tense, let alone jittery, is usually licked before he begins. He must have enough confidence in his case, and in his ability to present it, to enable him to conduct his side of the debate calmly and intelligently.

This in turn (as we shall have occasion to note repeatedly in the chapters ahead) means that he will have to know his case well enough to think about it clearly and express his thoughts about it with equal clarity.

Next, a person can and must acquire enough basic comprehension of logical processes to use them correctly and effectively. This needn't entail taking a college-level course in formal logic: On the contrary, that can be positively constipating in the rough-and-tumble of a typical informal argument. Luckily, most people learn, simply in the process of growing up and rattling around, that the fact that B happened after A doesn't necessarily prove that A caused B (the fallacy *post hoc ergo propter hoc*), or that the fact that A himself did the very thing for which he criticizes B doesn't necessarily justify B in doing it (*tu quoque*), even though it may debar A personally from criticizing him, etc.

Finally, one can acquire the sort of determination needed to enter, participate in, and win an argument. Once again it is largely a matter of confidence—but confidence based on sound training and, later, on growing experience.

Sure, some people are better "natural-born" arguers than others. We are dealing, after all, with a matter closely related to the subject of one's over-all personality. Some people are simply endowed with more natural force than others: One sees this in vivid operation in the case of a Napoleon or even a Hitler—short, not typically prepossessing men; yet when they entered a room even lifelong professional soldiers forgot their expertise and submitted to their innate authority.

In a much smaller way, some people use their natural gifts, often quite unconsciously, to win assent or overpower opposition to their desires. A person not so gifted can recognize that fact without crumpling before it, however, because arguing is far more a matter of acquired than innate skills. Properly trained, a person with no innate talent for arguing should be able to win quite a lot of his arguments, and to battle the world champion (whoever he or she is) to a draw 100 percent of the time.

That training is what this book proposes to give you. So don't be discouraged if arguing isn't your *forte*—even if you have lost again and again when you felt deep in your bones that you deserved to win. If you deserved to—believe me—you can.

V

THE BASIC PRINCIPLE OF
SUCCESSFUL ARGUMENTATION

Many people who are not competent arguers, especially those who (perhaps not realizing that fact) are forever getting into arguments anyway and losing, apparently think that winning an argument is basically just a matter of luck. Another large group realizes that there's more to it than luck, but secretly believes that those who defeat them are just a little more highly skilled in the black arts of oratorical trickery. Both groups are thus often tempted to "match with destiny for beers," on the theory that the odds are at least nearly even. Both are quite wrong, and the first major lesson in winning arguments is to understand this.

Luck or trickery may of course win an argument every now and then, but no serious and successful arguer would dream of relying on either for a moment. Instead, victory in the vast majority of arguments goes to the arguer who has most thoroughly analyzed the issue or issues, and has rooted his position in premises that are, for one reason or another, literally unassailable.

In a way, therefore, arguing is rather like playing chess: Victory belongs to the contestant who sees most deeply into the position. And since it is observable that in grandmaster chess there are a large number of draws (in Karpov's 1978 match with Korchnoi in Manila, the world championship was won 6 games to 5, with 21 draws!), it should not surprise us that between two competent arguers there will be far more contests fairly scored as "draws" than there will be victories legitimately assignable to either side.

Fortunately, however, the analogy to chess is imperfect because (among other things) chess masters generally look far deeper into the position, in terms of forseeable moves, than even the ablest arguers can or needs to. A better analogy to arguing, in many ways, is that childishly simple game, tick-tack-toe.

Is there anybody left who doesn't realize that a competent player simply cannot be beaten at tick-tack-toe?—that he will either win or draw, not merely most of the time but *always?* The point is easy to demonstrate. If our man makes the first move, he merely avoids putting his X in one of the corner squares. Any other square will do, e.g.:

At this point, his opponent is already doomed either to lose or (at best) draw. If he puts his mark in one of the corners of the same row:

—our man can force a draw by occupying the center square and the far corner in the same row as his opponent's first move:

If the opponent puts his mark in one of the corners of the far row, our man can still force a draw by occupying the center square and then the vacant far corner:

If the opponent puts his mark in the middle square of the row opposite our man's X, and our man occupies the center square on his second move, the opponent is again forced to draw by putting his second mark in a corner square or face disaster:

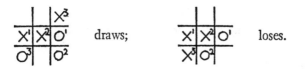

draws;   loses.

If the opponent puts his first mark in the center square, our man can similarly force a draw by occupying one of the far corner squares on his second move:

Conversely, if our man goes second he can always obtain a draw, either as above if his opponent proceeds as outlined above for the first move, or by taking care to occupy a *corner square* if his opponent's first move is to occupy the center square:

—or by taking care to occupy the center square and then a middle square, if his opponent opts to start from a corner:

In short, losing a game of tick-tack-toe is proof positive that the loser made a simple mistake of some sort; with a little foresight, it is *always* possible to draw, no matter how able one's opponent.

The beauty of arguing (and its attraction for many logical minds) is that precisely the same is true of an argument: *Properly conducted,* an argument should theoretically always end in, at worst, a draw—i.e., in a different evaluation of principles or an unresolvable disagreement as to the facts. If it doesn't end this way—if one side "wins"—that is invariably because the other side "made a wrong move," either at the outset or in the course of argumentation: i.e., relied upon either a principle or a key fact that the opposition was able to undermine.

An illustration even simpler than a game of tick-tack-toe will serve to illustrate the point. If Mr. Jones, looking up from his newspaper, says to his wife one evening, "Let's go out for a stroll," Mrs. Jones may say, "No," thus launching an argument—and then win it hands down by adding, "It's raining." In its simplest form, this was an argument won by the arguer in possession of superior relevant factual data. (Mr. Jones ought to have looked out the window first.)

If Mr. Jones gets stubborn and retorts, "I like it when it rains," Mrs. Jones may merely reply, "I don't." She has thereby exploited what proved to be Mr. Jones's further mistake in removing the whole controversy from the realm of objective fact to one of personal preference; she doesn't like rain, and it is a familiar principle that *de gustibus non est disputandum:* "There's no arguing over tastes."

Mr. Jones may try to get this mini-argument back on the track by contending that "Strolling in the rain is good for you"—and adducing as factual evidence an article he's read in the paper in which some doctor so asserts on allegedly scientific grounds. Mrs. Jones may let herself be persuaded by this new factual datum (in which case Mr. Jones "wins"), or she may successfully challenge its validity (citing an overwhelming number of cases, from William Henry Harrison on down, in which inclement weather proved fatal), or she may just elect to stand on her own preference in the matter. In the first of the latter two situations, Mr. Jones loses on factual grounds again; in the second, he loses because of the principle that his preference has no higher standing than his wife's.

Simple as it is, this little contretemps illustrates the basic structure of most, if not all, arguments: A case to be argued pro and con; the declaration of relevant principles; the bringing forward of factual

data relevant to an intelligent decision in the matter; and the ultimate resolution of the controversy, either by the presentation of superior principles and/or facts, or by the reduction of the argument to
a level invulnerable to either.

Of course, most arguments are at least slightly more complicated
than the above, but their complexity lies only in their heavier burden
of relevant principles and/or factual data. An excellent example of
an argument involving an almost inconceivably large and complex
array of relevant factual data is the one over the SALT II treaty.

The SALT II argument is particularly interesting because both
sides shared the same basic principle: A treaty with the Soviet
Union limiting strategic arms in a balanced fashion would be desirable, but the security of the United States must be protected at all
costs in any treaty entered into. There are, to be sure, positions at
odds with this one, at both extremes of the political spectrum. Some
conservatives would argue quite seriously that the United States simply ought never, purely as a matter of morality (i.e., principle), to
enter into a treaty with a Communist power. On the other hand,
there are unilateral disarmament advocates (I once actually met
one) who favor the United States jettisoning its whole armory of
offensive and defensive weapons, in the serene confidence that this
would so assuage the fears of the Soviet Union that it would follow
suit. We may disagree with either or both of these positions, but
there isn't much point to arguing over them; like Mrs. Jones's distaste
for rain, they do not respond to disagreement—they simply defy it.
The argument would in either case theoretically end in a draw, save
that the extreme nature of the conservative's principle and the child-
ish quality of the unilateralist's faith will, in the eyes of many, put
their holders out of court.

(This reminds us, incidentally, that it is usually not sufficient to
beat a retreat to just any old principle or alleged fact, and claim
thereby a technical draw in the argument, if the object of the argument in question is to "win" by convincing some third individual or
group—e.g., in the case of SALT II, the U. S. Senate. The principle
itself must have a fair amount of appeal; the fact—or, in the case of
the unilateralist, the prediction—must have some credibility. If Mr.
and Mrs. Jones had submitted their dispute to some third party,

Mrs. Jones's dislike for strolling in the rain might well be scored as reasonable enough to result in more than a merely technical victory.)

Fortunately, in the case of SALT II, proponents and opponents were very largely agreed upon the basic need for U.S. security under any treaty. This shifted the whole argument onto a purely factual plane, which (as noted) involved an almost infinite array of relevant factual data. Under the treaty as proposed, critics objected that the Soviet Union seemed to have an advantage in this or that category. Proponents of the treaty would respond by pointing out factors that, in one way or another, appeared to cancel or counter the advantage. Critics would then object to the empirical verifiability of some of these factors. And so on. It is hard not to feel a certain sympathy for the members of the Senate, who had to decide where truth—and hence security—lay in this tangle of technical military data, always remembering to resolve bottom-line uncertainties *against* ratification.

Luckily, few if any of the arguments in which the average man or woman becomes involved are quite as complex, in factual terms, as the argument over SALT II. But most serious arguments do entail disagreements on matters of fact, and winning an argument therefore usually involves knowing how to marshal and offer factual evidence in support of your position. Conversely, you must be prepared to counter factual data offered by your opponent—either by attacking them directly (as wrong) or indirectly (as irrelevant). In terms of our simple illustration, Mr. Jones might be able to respond to Mrs. Jones's "It's raining" with either a superior factual barrage ("It stopped raining an hour ago and the stars are out") or by demonstrating that Mrs. Jones's factual objection ("It's raining") may be true enough but is irrelevant. (Hard to do in the Joneses' case, but perhaps they have a large estate with a long sheltered walkway down to the greenhouse, or something of that sort; in such a case, Mrs. Jones's factual objection might be demonstrably irrelevant.)

The mistake most people make, however, is to rush into an argument without being sufficiently sure of the factual support for the position they have taken—or, for that matter, of the soundness of the principles underlying it. Putting it another way, they undertake to argue cases that no really competent arguer would touch with a ten-foot pole. Either they are carried away by their own ill-advised enthusiasm for the point they wish to argue, or they simply gamble that their opponent will not have the factual or philosophical artillery to gun them down. This is roughly as sensible as attacking a burglar on the chance that he isn't armed.

What the above boils down to is a rule absolutely basic to winning arguments: *Never undertake to argue a case whose fundamental principles and factual support are not known to you, in advance, to be sufficient to guarantee either victory or, at the very least, a draw.*

Winning an argument, then, is not, or at any rate ought not to be, even slightly a matter of luck or trickery. Every case involves basically two types of argumentation: Argumentation based upon fundamental principles of one sort or another (which, if valid and applicable, must prevail, and whose validity and applicability are thus the only directions from which they can be attacked), and argumentation based upon relevant factual data (which similarly can be attacked as either inaccurate or irrelevant). The competent arguer will have analyzed the structure of his case, and will know which basic principles he proposes to rest it on, and what factual data are available in its support. This will automatically tell him what the weak points of his case are—and, of course, both the weak and strong points of the opposition. To the extent that he can, he will seek to eliminate any weak points in his own case; if he cannot do so to a sufficient extent, he will modify or if necessary abandon the case at the outset, rather than lose the argument once it has begun.

A competent arguer, therefore, is entitled to feel a certain serenity before the argument even begins. That is because the argument he has chosen to enter is one he understands fully, and whose conduct he is prepared for, with sufficient factual support or (if the facts do not point definitively in any one direction) on the basis of valid and applicable principles.

Between two adversaries, without the need to persuade a third party, the facts alone may do the job: i.e., convince an opponent who started out feeling otherwise. If they don't—if the Battle of the Facts is inconclusive—then the argument will usually end in an "agreement to disagree," since neither side will ordinarily yield on its principles.

Where there is a third party to be persuaded, the facts may (again) be decisive; but if they are not, then everything is likely to depend on how the third party evaluates the respective first principles appealed to. Here again, the competent arguer will be confident of the broad appeal (to the third party) of the principles on which he bases his case.

Like the competent tick-tack-toe player, the competent arguer has left nothing to chance: He enters the arena knowing—and chooses in advance only arenas where he knows—that he can either win or draw.

But how does he choose the arena?

VI

DEFINING THE ISSUE

If choosing the position wisely is the key to successful argumentation, then defining the issue is the first and most important step in the argumentation process itself: i.e., in the communications between the arguers. It is probable that a full 90 percent of all arguments are for all practical purposes over when this step has been completed: At that point, whether his opponent realizes it or not, the competent arguer has taken his stand on territory he knows to be impregnable. His principles are valid and applicable; his facts are relevant and true. All that remains is to ascertain how well his opponent has chosen. If wisely, the argument is bound to end in what amounts to a draw—usually a difference of opinion as to which of two valid principles ought to prevail over the other. If unwisely, then our competent arguer will swiftly exploit the weaknesses in his opponent's position, and win. Defining the issue, therefore, is obviously crucial.

A good many years ago, when the controversy over the Communist Party, the John Birch Society, etc. was at its peak, an organization in New York City inquired whether I would be willing to debate Jacob Javits, the liberal Republican senator from New York, on the general subject. I replied that I would be happy to do so. Further negotiations through intermediaries revealed that Javits too was not unwilling, provided the topic was, "Is the Hard Right a Danger to America?"—with Javits presumably taking the affirmative, and me the negative.

Probably a good many people would have accepted that formulation of the topic—with fatal results. For it permitted only two possible outcomes: Either the hard right *was* a danger to America (in which case Javits won), or it wasn't—it was by implication merely a minor factor, whether malignant or benign, of no importance in any case. In the latter event, for all practical purposes, Javits at worst would have achieved something like a draw, and in a sense might even be said to have "won." Heads he won, tails I lost! Or, to put it in football terms, it was to be agreed in advance that the whole debate would take place between the 50-yard line and my end zone. Javits could score if he was able or lucky enough. I couldn't possibly do better than hold him scoreless.

Accordingly, I responded by declining to debate the proposed topic, but offered to debate instead the following question: "Is the Hard Right or Hard Left the Greater Danger to America?" This was far more evenly balanced, since it gave me an equal chance to go over to the offensive: to carry the war into Javits' territory, so to speak, by contending that the hard left was a greater danger than the hard right. Javits promptly declined to debate this topic—proving, whatever else it demonstrated, that he understood very well the difference between a balanced question and a lopsided pushover.

On another occasion about that same time, a college Young Republican Club on a Long Island campus asked me if I would agree to debate some liberal (to be recruited later) on that campus during Academic Freedom Week. I said I would, and noted the proposed date on my calendar. In a few days the YR's were back on the phone, with the good news that a suitable opponent had been found. "The topic," the young man on the phone told me, "will be 'Academic Freedom.' He will take the affirmative, and you will take the negative."

"Whoa!" I practically shouted. "I'll do no such thing. I'm not against academic freedom, and I don't know any conservative who is. The question up for discussion these days is, *how much* academic freedom? Or some variation of that theme. For example, should an avowed (or unavowed) Communist be permitted to teach?" Eventually a formulation was agreed on, but here again note how nearly I was maneuvered—in all innocence, I am sure, as far as the YR sponsors were concerned—into agreeing to defend an indefensible position.

It is absolutely fascinating to see how woozily many people approach the formulation of interesting and important questions. Not too long ago former Senator Eugene McCarthy and I were asked to debate at a well-known southern college on the topic, "The United States in the 1980s." I promptly called Gene and teasingly proposed that I take the affirmative: "I'll be *for* the United States in the 1980s. You be against it." But Gene wasn't so easily lured. We discussed ways of reshaping the topic so as to produce a balanced debate. I suggested, in view of the obvious typecasting by our hosts, that we might argue "Is Liberalism or Conservatism the Best Course for the United States in the 1980s?" I felt perfectly at home with that formulation, but Gene didn't. Whatever his position had been in the mid-1960s, he did not now want to be charged with the task of recommending liberalism, pure and simple, as the course for America in the 1980s. Finally we agreed to discuss, "Is Conservatism the Best Course for America in the 1980s?" In a sense McCarthy (as he conceded) would have the better side of this issue, since I would be committed to arguing for a particular viewpoint, with all the accompanying dangers of seeming narrow, puristic, and rigidly ideological, whereas Gene could attack me from any direction or combination of directions he chose, including (but not exclusively confined to) liberalism. But I felt this disadvantage was partially counterbalanced by having the entire battlefield shifted, so to speak, in my direction. I was in this respect in roughly the same position Senator Javits had· sought to achieve for himself: The whole game would be played between the 50-yard line and my opponent's end zone. McCarthy might have acquired all the advantages of a defensive stance, but it was hard to see how he could score affirmatively. My own biggest danger, plainly, would be that implication of rigid ideological purity in my own stance; I would have to overcome it by tonal stresses on my reasonableness.

Of course, when a sponsor proposes a debate on "The United States in the 1980s" he often is not contemplating a debate *per se*. If pressed, he will frequently reply that he hadn't really intended to have "a formal *debate*" (an *argument*, for heaven's sake!), but rather something more like a *panel* or a *discussion*—trusting to the well known (or at least assumed) differences between McCarthy's general views and mine to produce a peppery touch of disagreement.

When I encounter that sort of response, I know I am in the presence of another example of our current national distaste for outright assertions. The same frame of mind that precedes every statement with the softening, pseudo-similizing "Like," and accompanies it with an ingratiating "you know," shrinks from "a formal debate" in which two worthy opponents square off and take precisely opposite sides of a carefully formulated question. But, as the last chapter demonstrated, muddled thinking is not really an effective lubricant for differences of opinion. Far more disagreements arise *from* muddled thinking than are ever resolved *by* it.

That is why the old research director of General Motors, Charles F. "Boss" Kettering, was fond of saying, "A problem well stated is a problem half solved." In pure logic, that is technically not true: Posing a question well may prepare it for solution, much as a patient in a hospital is carefully prepared for an operation, but it doesn't even begin the actual process of solving it. Nonetheless, experience had taught Kettering that an imprecise verbal formulation of a problem could be a deadly obstacle to what might otherwise be a comparatively simple solution.

An amusing historical episode will serve to illustrate this point. In the nineteenth century Britain spent a good deal of blood and treasure trying to force China, under its Manchu dynasty, to accept commercial and other relations. The Chinese fought back stubbornly. In her excellent book, *The Dragon Empress*, Marina Warner somewhere remarks that the collision between the two great empires rested on mutual misconceptions: The British, drawing on their experience of "lesser breeds," insisted on treating the Chinese as colonials, while the Chinese, accustomed to thinking of China as "the Central Kingdom," regarded the British as rebels. There never was, and in the circumstances probably could not be, a mutually agreed upon and accurate *statement of the problem*, which was that a technologically advanced European power in the flood tide of its vigor was seeking highly lucrative commercial prerogatives in a China ruled by a corrupt and decaying dynasty. But if there had been, it might have helped to solve the problem.

Fortunately, most arguments that the average person is likely to get into are more susceptible of an agreed and precise formulation.

Without it, many a "panel discussion" drifts into a limbo where the participants find they agree on all basic points (which is supposed to be good) and the audience slowly falls asleep (which is plainly bad). Without it, in fact, many arguments—especially the kind that threaten to end in lawsuits—preoccupy the arguers through long days or even years, with correspondingly high costs of one sort or another.

From time to time, of course, the sheer vagueness of a topic will be used by one of the arguers as a sort of refuge. Unable or unwilling to defend any given position, he takes the field in the hope that it will remain shrouded in the dialectical equivalent of a pea-soup fog, in which with a little agility he can remain present, yet intact.

For all of these reasons, the competent arguer will insist upon its being decided, at the very outset, precisely what position he himself is to argue for—and he will also insist, at least in most cases, upon knowing exactly what position his adversary is undertaking to defend. A few examples, drawn from the sixty "Advocates" programs in which I have participated, will illustrate some of the problems that can arise.

"The Advocates" is, of course, the well known hour-long discussion program that flourished on the Public Broadcasting System from 1969–1974, was revived in 1978, and has been visible on PBS, at least occasionally, each season since then. I was the regular advocate for the conservative position on public issues from 1970–73 (my liberal opponent usually being Howard Miller, later president of the Los Angeles Board of Education), and have appeared intermittently in subsequent seasons. "The Advocates" is a superb training ground for the arts of argumentation, but the program is assuredly no place for an amateur.

The format is, very loosely, that of a courtroom, in which some public issue is in effect litigated. There is a "moderator" (corresponding to the judge) and two "advocates" (the attorneys), who call "witnesses" (lay experts on the subject). When the program is over the television audience (the jury) is invited to send in its verdict on the issue. The two advocates are not necessarily in fact lawyers (and indeed cannot be so described, in deference to the sensibilities of the legal profession), but they very often are, as one might expect on a program devoted to systematic argumentation.

In view of what has already been said about the importance of defining the issue, the reader can safely assume that I always gave my most careful attention to the phraseology of the question to be debated. Both Miller and I badly wanted to win, and a tremendous amount depended on what we were forced—or could force each other—to contend. It was nothing unusual for us to haggle for hours over the exact wording of a question—face to face, then by phone with each other and the producers of the show (who, I am sure, thought we were both demented), and often face to face yet again. Both being lawyers, we saw many things alike—even to sharing very often the same assessment of some proposed topic's possibilities and dangers. Luckily, there was usually no problem in finding a "basis of disagreement," so to speak. I was and still am, inside and out, Central Casting's notion of the prototypical conservative; Miller was (I cannot speak for him today) a liberal of hue so pure and unpolluted that I often suspected he spent his nights sleeping under a bell jar in the National Bureau of Standards. It was tacitly understood that neither of us would be required to defend any position with which we felt uncomfortable.

It was the almost invariable practice of "The Advocates," I guess for the purposes of uniformity and focus, to phrase every question in the form of a proposal for some form of government action: e.g., "Should the Federal Government register voters for Presidential elections?" or "Should Congress approve import quotas on textiles and shoes?" In a way, this custom itself skewed the program in favor of an activist government: We were always debating whether government ought to be doing something *more*—usually something brand-new—with comparatively little chance to discuss whether it ought to be doing *less*.

Nevertheless, the formula at least tended to focus the debate on something concrete. "Should America have national health insurance?" would have been a hopelessly vague topic: what kind of insurance? how much of it? paid for by whom? insured by whom? But "Should the Federal Government guarantee comprehensive medical care for all Americans?" is a good deal better, and when it is agreed (as it was, on the program on this subject) that the two sides would confine themselves to debating the Kennedy-Corman Bill, one had, whether pro or con, something specific to grapple with.

Glancing over a list of the long series of questions I debated, I note that one of the most important by-products of a particular form of a question was to determine who had the affirmative and thus went first. Going first can be useful or not, depending on circumstances; but on a program that is forever asking whether government ought to do something new, the conservative advocate is obviously likely to wind up taking the negative far more often than not. As the negative side began, in my first season (1970–71), to win what the show's producers deemed an inordinate number of the debates—at least as determined by the votes of the TV audience—they began tinkering with the questions to try to make sure that I was obliged to take the affirmative occasionally. Their working hypothesis was that there might be some hitherto undiscovered disadvantage to having the affirmative of a proposal *per se*. (Perhaps people were just naturally more *agin* than *fer*.) I am happy to report that when the producers commissioned an objective study of this possibility, their analyst glumly reported that while the negative did indeed seem to have a mysterious inherent advantage, it was markedly less when I was assigned to the affirmative.

In any event, the list of topics demonstrates how readily interchangeable the affirmative and negative sides of a question often are.

"Should Congress approve import quotas on textiles and shoes?" gives the affirmative (including the right to go first) to the side defending quotas. "Should Congress reject [or eliminate] import quotas on textiles and shoes?" reverses the roles, giving the opponent of quotas the affirmative. Usually, though, it is considered bad form —or at least stylistically lazy—to produce the opposite result merely by replacing the word "approve" with a word such as "reject." This is because what might be called the "true affirmative" on such an issue is whatever proposes a change from the status quo. If, at the time of the debate, there are no quotas on textiles and shoes, then the "true affirmative" is the side that proposes such quotas. If, therefore, there is some compelling reason for wanting the other side to have the affirmative, it is usually best to revamp the entire question, as in, "Would import quotas on textiles and shoes injure the U.S. economy?" This gives the quota opponent a more genuine affirmative, and enables him to lead off with a sonorous hymn to the (affirmative) concept of the free market, which import quotas to some extent necessarily violate. Even then, however, since the affirmative is the defender of the status quo (assuming there are, in fact, no such quotas), a strong case can be made that the negative's advocate has the "true affirmative" side of the question. However, lifting the whole issue to a higher plane (e.g., "Is a free market basically preferable to a protected one?") would give the opponent of quotas the "true affirmative." It involves a clash of principles in which neither side necessarily represents the status quo, but the quota foe's answer to the question as phrased is, "Yes" (i.e., affirmative). But "The Advocates'" preference for debating concrete proposals for change usually prevented it from raising the discussion to such rarefied levels.

Of course, if import quotas on shoes and textiles actually exist at the time of the debate, the roles are reversed and the opponent of such quotas, as the supporter of a change in the status quo, has the "true affirmative."

Occasionally a proposal for a change in the status quo gives the affirmative to a basically negative position. This was the case when "The Advocates" decided to debate the Daniel Ellsberg ("Pentagon Papers") problem. The question could theoretically have been put in many ways: "Was Ellsberg justified in handing over the Pentagon Papers to the press?" "Should security take precedence over the people's right to know?" "Should the Government have prosecuted Ellsberg?" Etc. Since Ellsberg's prosecution was already under way, however, the program inquired more topically, "Should the Government drop the charges against Daniel Ellsberg?"—thus giving the affirmative to the side that was surely closer to the "true negative," since it opposed Ellsberg's prosecution.

Then there are topics that can be put either way with equal propriety. "Should strikers be denied welfare benefits?" might just as easily have been phrased, "Should strikers be entitled to welfare benefits?" Both formulations were about equally fair and justifiable in terms of the status quo, since at the time of the debate roughly twenty large and heavily industrialized states allowed such benefits to strikers, while some thirty smaller states didn't.

The pitfalls in defining the issue are by no means behind us, however, when we have finally agreed on which side has the affirmative and therefore should go first. Take the question debated on "The Advocates" in March 1972: "Should the Constitution be amended to prohibit the assignment of school children on the basis of race?" This was less than a year after the Supreme Court had sanctioned forced busing to facilitate the assignment of children to specific schools on the basis of their race, and the affirmative of the proposition was thus maintained by the side that opposed forced busing. But if the selfsame question had been debated prior to the Supreme Court's 1954 decision in *Brown* vs. *Board of Education*, it would have seemed clear that liberals favored the affirmative, since the whole thrust of that momentous decision was to bar the assignment of school children on the basis of race. The intervening two decades had carried the liberal viewpoint forward to a new position that was the exact opposite of the one previously held. This caused no confusion in 1972, but the same question, debated (say) in 1962 or 1968, might have presented serious questions of basic meaning.

Every now and then the formulation of a question may include words that, deliberately or otherwise, to some degree slant the question rhetorically. That seemed—and still seems—to me to be the trouble with, "Should large corporations be driven out of farming?" which "The Advocates" debated in 1972. The basic question was a perfectly legitimate one: whether large corporations ("agribusiness") ought to be permitted to engage in farming, or whether farming ought to be confined by law to relatively small enterprises: individual families and small corporations. It was, so to speak, the agricultural equivalent of the old philosophical dispute over supermarkets versus corner grocery stores.

But why "driven out"? The phrase unnecessarily (and in my opinion unjustifiably) brought to mind the image of Jesus driving the money-changers from the Temple. One could just as easily have asked, "Should large corporations be prohibited from engaging in farming?" and avoided the pejorative tone. It is impossible to know how many viewers, asked to vote on the question, found themselves tempted toward the affirmative (which won the postcard tally) by that vigorous, subtly righteous formulation. On the other hand, it is true that some viewers may have been turned off by it. In fairness to the producers of the show, I should stress that I am sure their use of that particular formulation was determined only by what they felt was its commendably theatrical ring.

One of the most important steps in formulating any issue is, of course, defining any potentially ambiguous terms that are employed in the formulation. "If you would argue with me, define your terms," said Socrates, and the old gentleman knew what he was talking about. In even the simplest argument it will pay to make sure that the key words mean the same thing to everyone. What, for example, does "immediately" mean? Added to the sentence, "What I need is a drink," it probably means within half an hour at the outside; added to, "This country should build a nuclear aircraft carrier," it obviously deals in many months, if not years.

On one occasion "The Advocates" decided to devote two successive programs to the question of U.S. policy toward South Africa. The formulation of one obvious question presented no particular problem: "Should the U.S. discourage investment in South Africa?" But the producers also wanted to discuss apartheid in one way or another. The problem was that the word "apartheid" is used in this country to refer promiscuously to either of two quite different things: the numerous policies of the South African Government that mandate racial segregation in living quarters, schools, jobs, etc., and the specific plan of the South African Government to promote "separate homelands" for the nine major black tribes, each of which is ultimately envisioned under the plan as becoming a technically sovereign and independent nation. (Four—the Transkei, Bophutatswana, Venda and Ciskei—have, in fact, subsequently done so.)

Now, one may oppose one of these policies or both (or I suppose theoretically neither). The great majority of Americans today, surely, would oppose the former, and there is certainly a powerful case to be made against the latter. But there is also a perfectly respectable and by no means necessarily "racist" case to be made in *favor* of the latter—i.e., in favor of the basic concept of "separate development" of the races in South Africa, either along the lines laid down by the present government or along other lines more generous in their provision for the country's blacks.

But whatever one is for or against, there was certainly no point to trying to debate these two quite different policies in one hour-long program. In addition, the present climate of American opinion made a debate on the merits of segregation in daily life almost pointless— that policy has virtually no public support in the United States today. Far more debatable, in the sense of having more to be said for both sides, was the question of the "separate homelands" policy. But how could this be discussed as a distinct issue without abandoning the word "apartheid," which the show's producers understandably wanted to retain in the title because of its established ability to attract attention and arouse controversy?

Fortunately, there was solution, based on South Africa's own experience in using the term. Where the context doesn't make plain which policy is being referred to, South Africans themselves refer to the various policies of racial segregation in daily living as "petty apartheid," and call the "separate homelands" policy "grand apartheid." So the question, as finally formulated on "The Advocates," was: "Is grand apartheid a policy worthy of U.S. support?" This still reflected the producers' preference for posing questions in terms of U. S. Government policy, whereas actually the issue of the desirability or non-desirability of grand apartheid is perfectly debatable without using that particular peg. But the unnecessary accretion did no particular harm, and the question was also vindicated as legitimately debatable when more than a third of the TV audience who voted cast ballots marked, "Yes."

I have already touched, in discussing the perils of misformulation, on the way in which a particular formulation of a question may shift the ground on which combat can take place toward or away from your own (or your adversary's) objective. Senator Javits, offering in the early 1960s to debate, "Is the Hard Right a Danger to America?" was seeking to focus the discussion on the perils of the hard right and spare himself any obligation to defend or minimize the hard left. In my debate with Gene McCarthy on "Is Conservatism the Course for the U.S. in the 1980s?" I waived any comparable right to belabor the liberal alternative because I was confident that I could

make an appealing case for conservatism—whereas I had no intention or desire to make one for right-wing extremism. It is time, however, to note more generally what these illustrations have already
demonstrated: i.e., that one extremely important aspect of defining
any issue for the purpose of debating it is to agree on what a proposed formulation permits, and does not permit, to be discussed.

The point can arise in a family context just as easily as in the
offices of "The Advocates." Traveling in Argentina some years ago, I
met a charming Midwestern couple in their 60s who had only begun
traveling extensively late in life. I asked the lady how she came to
choose Argentina as a destination. "Well," she replied with a twin-
kle, "two years ago when we first decided we could afford to travel,
my husband asked me, 'Would you rather go to England or South
America?' I chose England. Last year he asked me, 'Would you
rather go to western Europe or South America?'—and I chose western Europe. This year he asked me, 'How would you like to come to
South America with me?'"

Her husband clearly knew how to formulate a question so as to
narrow the options effectively!

On a different level, a friend told me back in the 1950s, "When
the drive opens to recognize Red China, those favoring it will put
the question this way: 'Should our policy toward China be flexible or
inflexible?'" Thus put, it is almost impossible to give any reply but
the obvious one—the question is virtually rhetorical. An opponent of
recognition, tilting the pinball machine equally far in the other direction, might have suggested debating, "Shall our policy toward China
be governed by principle or expediency?"

Of course, in the case of "The Advocates" or similar relatively formal debates, the sheer need to publicize the event in advance will
often almost compel a reasonably fair and precise formulation of the
question at the very outset of planning. In less formal arguments,
however—e.g., in the home or office—the dispute will often arise in
ways that do not call insistently for such a formulation. In that case
the parties may overlook this important detail altogether—only to
discover, hours or days later—that they have been "talking at cross-
purposes": i.e., have fundamentally misunderstood each other's contention (rather like the two deaf Englishmen on the bus: "I say, is

this Wembley?" "No, this is Thursday." "By Jove, so am I! Let's get off and have a drink.").

One therefore should always take care to attend to this matter of issue definition, even in the humblest argument. The clarifying question is usually put in some such way as, "Are you saying . . ." (or, more aggressively, "Do you mean to tell me . . ."), or "Is it your contention . . ." A little care of this sort at the outset can often save a great deal of time—or even avert an argument altogether.

VII

THRESHOLD CONSIDERATIONS

Assuming that the question has been precisely formulated, the competent arguer will next turn to various strategic considerations that must receive attention at the very outset.

WHAT IS THE PURPOSE OF THIS PARTICULAR ARGUMENT?

Up until now we have assumed that unless an arguer is merely trying to work off his aggressions or clarify an issue, his purpose, broadly speaking, is "to win"—or, putting it a little more cautiously, "to prevail." But "winning" or "prevailing" can mean many things.

Let me offer an illustration. In the mid-1960s I accepted an invitation to debate a well known anti-war activist on the general subject of the Vietnam war, before the Yale Political Union. It was to be my first appearance before that venerable organization, and I knew relatively little about its procedures. Unlike my colleague Bill Buckley, I had not attended Yale; my undergraduate work was done at Princeton, and for my law school I chose Harvard.

I had heard somewhere, however, that the Union was officially divided among various "parties": the Liberal Democrats, the Liberals, the Independents, the Conservatives, and the Party of the Right. So when at the opening of the meeting the presiding officer called for a vote of the members of the Union on the question we were about to debate, I felt no pain: No sixth sense warned me that there was something a little odd about calling for a vote *before* hearing the arguments.

To tell the truth, I was looking forward eagerly to that particular debate. I have forgotten the precise formulation of the question, but whatever it was I felt sure I had a strong case and could do a good job. Moreover my opponent, I happened to know, was no great shakes as a debater. I was anticipating some fun at his expense—a little light sarcasm, perhaps; a particularly scathing rebuttal; in general, a performance that, however much they might disagree with me, would show the Yalies that Bill Buckley wasn't the only deadly debater at *National Review*.

It all worked precisely as I had planned. My opponent plodded patiently and politely from point to point; I danced around him like Bugs Bunny—spearing him in unexpected places, tripping him when he turned to confront his tormentor, and then patronizing him when he fell. I knew my performance was bound to be a bit irritating; but I also knew it was clever, and I saw no reason not to be clever.

Until, that is, the debate was over and the presiding officer called for a *second vote* on the question we had debated! That, I suddenly realized with an awful sinking feeling, was standard procedure at the Union: to vote on a topic both before and after it had been debated, to determine which debater had been more persuasive. I kept a sort of sickly grin on my face as the second vote was taken. As I well knew would be the case in the circumstances, the number of Union members supporting my side of the argument was perceptibly lower —not overwhelmingly, but perceptibly. Even among my stalwart allies in the Conservative Party and the Party of the Right, there were defections. I had, in effect, lost the debate.

And I had lost it simply because *I had not paid attention to the special meaning of "winning" under the rules of the Yale Political Union*. Under proper circumstances there is not necessarily anything wrong with the sort of debate I chose to conduct at Yale: a slashing, taunting attack. It does, of course, annoy some people (while delighting others); but persuading people is not always a matter of wooing them with honeyed words. If the position they espouse on a given issue is exposed to truly effective ridicule, for example, they may hate the person who ridicules it, but they may also, later and very quietly, move away from the position that has been demonstrated to be ridiculous. (We shall return to this point later.)

But however justifiable my strategy might have been under other circumstances, it was totally *un*justifiable under the circumstances obtaining at the Yale Political Union. When in Rome, do as the Romans do; and my job that fatal day had been to win the sympathy of the audience, both intellectually and emotionally, and thus persuade a handful who had voted the other way at the outset to change their votes as a result of my argumentation. I had failed utterly to do this; worse, I hadn't even tried.

By way of defense, let me say that I do not always behave like a spoiled brat in a debate. Not long after that disastrous encounter at Yale I was again asked to debate the Vietnam war, this time on the University of California's Berkeley campus. Berkeley, of course, was widely and rightly regarded in those days as a hotbed of student leftism. To make matters worse, if possible, my opponent was to be a member of Berkeley's own faculty: a popular advocate of all the prevailing leftist causes. It seemed probable that I would be lucky if I managed to leave the campus without being tarred and feathered. I knew it was a tough assignment, and I laid my plans with care.

When my talk was over, I got a standing ovation from the audience of approximately a thousand Berkeley students—and they were not a bunch of Milquetoasts, either. But this time I had correctly assessed the audience, the circumstances, and my relation to both. My talk was low-keyed, reasonable, concessive; I pled for understanding, and ostentatiously looked for common ground. In my conclusion, I have forgotten whether my analogy to Luther's dilemma before the Diet of Worms was expressed or implied, but the message was plain: Here I stand. I cannot do otherwise. God help me. Amen.

I once saw Bill Buckley learn, even more spectacularly, from a mistake comparable to the one I made at Yale. In 1965 he agreed to debate the noted black author James Baldwin before the Cambridge Union on the subject, "Resolved, that the American Dream is at the expense of the American Negro." Buckley had attended prep school in England and was well aware of the formula for success before the Union: One is witty, very lightly sarcastic, and if possible subtly devastating. Unlike the Yale Political Union, the Cambridge Union takes no "before" and "after" votes for comparison; but it does vote on the question after the debaters have spoken, and the vote is clearly understood as registering the sense of the audience as to the skill of the debaters quite as much as to the merits of the issue.

The event was filmed and subsequently broadcast, so I was able to watch it. Buckley was everything a classical debater before the Union was supposed to be: He scintillated as only Buckley can scintillate. James Baldwin—slight of stature, ugly, and solemn—did not attempt to compete with Bill; instead he sought—successfully on this occasion—to transcend him. He spoke, in the tones of the great writer he is, of the agony and fury of America's blacks. When both men had finished, the Cambridge Union voted, by a margin of 3 to 1, for Baldwin's side of the question.

But that is only the first half of the story. Later that year Buckley was again matched against Baldwin, this time on David Susskind's "Open End" television program. This time the topic was the abuses of police power—and this time Bill was ready. Again one heard, from Baldwin, the great organ tones of a deeply frustrated people. But from Buckley now there were no witticisms; only the deadly moral earnestness of a man who knew this was no time for flippancy. When the smoke blew away, Buckley was incontestably the victor.

In none of these instances, either those involving me or those involving Buckley, am I suggesting that there was even a trace of insincerity on our part. In each case it was simply a matter of appreciating, or failing to appreciate, the type of rhetorical approach appropriate to the subject, the opponent, and the audience. We all can approach most subjects in a variety of moods; what I have been trying to convey is the importance of the choice. It is one aspect of the over-all subject of this section: What does "winning" mean?

To a politician, to take another and quite different example, "winning" an argument may have almost nothing whatever to do with being seen to be right. I am not suggesting that politicians are always and everywhere indifferent to the correctness of their contentions; but quite a few of them are, and certainly many a successful political career has been built on intellectual foundations that wouldn't survive even a casual inspection. In his encounters with the public in pursuit of votes, at any rate, a politician's normal first concern must be to look and sound appealing, whether his statements actually make sense or not. As a Kentucky friend of mine once said of the late Senator Alben Barkley, "Senator Barkley was born with a worried look on his face, and he has managed to convince the people of Kentucky that what he's worried about is the state of the nation." Not a bad platform, as far as it went!

It is sometimes argued that, with increasing voter sophistication and the obligation to confront articulate opponents or interviewers in television debates or panels, it is harder for demagogues to fool the public than it used to be. Perhaps so; certainly some of the demagogues of yesteryear would be seen through easily today. But they were yesterday's demagogues, and I sometimes suspect that to-day's more sophisticated voters are simply being taken into camp by more sophisticated demagogues. "Cotton Ed" Smith might not get very far today, trying to "wave the bloody shirt" before Confederate nostalgiacs in South Carolina, but racism (and now, of course, "re-verse racism") is still being successfully appealed to in this country.

The competent arguer, then, will be on guard against the oppo-nent who intends to "win" demagogically by somehow engaging the sympathies of the audience without tossing more than a perfunctory nod toward the real issues. One recently defeated Midwestern sena-tor was an especially skilled performer of this sort. I once heard him make a speech in which, at one time or another, he identified him-self with almost every controversial figure in national politics. En-dorsing some view, he would assert, "Now that's where I agree with Barry Goldwater." A couple of minutes later, adopting some other stance, he would say, "Now there I agree with George McGovern." And so on. By the time he was through, he had managed to identify himself with just about everybody's particular hero on one point or another, while simultaneously impressing his listeners as a free spirit who wore no man's collar and who bravely refused to be bound by any narrow ideology. The fact that the resulting bouillabaisse of posi-tions was necessarily self-contradictory and often downright incoher-ent hardly mattered; the occasion was not a debate, so there was (as he knew there would be) no one to point this out.

Whether one is in politics or not, however, it may someday be-come important to "win" by persuading an audience, or a fraction of an audience, to take some particular action. Note that word "frac-tion," by the way. It isn't always, or even usually, necessary to convince *everybody*. In amending the by-laws of an organization, two thirds may be enough. In most other cases, a simple majority will do. If you oppose that by-law amendment, a mere one third plus one will defeat it. And there are situations—for example, on a jury— where even a single convert may be all you need.

A successful strategy, then, always takes note of the objective: whether to demolish the opposition simply as a logical exercise, or to persuade a given fraction of a group to take some desired action, or whatever. And the competent arguer will be on the alert for opponents who hope to win without addressing the real issues at all—i.e., by one or another form of sheer demagogy.

One other thought in this connection. It often happens, especially in arguing matters of public concern, that the target audience will already, by and large, have made up its mind. Each of two opposing debaters will naturally hope to win recruits to his viewpoint; but if one of them knows that a majority of the audience is on his side, logically his first concern will be to reinforce the loyalty of that majority. And this may lead to forms of argumentation quite different from those he would employ if he were seeking *primarily* to enlarge his following.

That brings us again to the fundamental question of how much winning an argument has to do with simply *being liked*, and—since it will recur in one form or another throughout this volume—we might as well confront and answer it here.

The answer, it has always seemed to me, depends (as so often) on the anterior question we have already discussed: What do we mean by "winning"? If the objective is to achieve some quick result—to induce a particular action, or even simply rouse an immediate sense of approbation and identification—then the competent arguer will say and do things that will cause him to be liked by his opponent or the audience, even at the technical expense of his argument. He may omit certain points because they might be offensive to some; he may concede others that are valid but not central to his case, just to seem "reasonable"; he will carefully avoid ridiculing even the patently ridiculous, or slapping down with full force some fallacious argument offered by his opponent. All this is quite proper. But pulling one's punches may also have the side effect of letting falsehood off too easily for the audience's (or even the opponent's) long-range good. One may win an argument today by exciting personal admiration or gratitude or even sympathy; but arguments "won" in this way tend to get lost retroactively. When the admired personality is gone and his charm has worn off, the fallacious arguments of his opponent which he treated so gently may reestablish themselves in the minds he (temporarily) changed. Or worse yet, the minds he changed may remain changed, but furnished with only a portion of the arsenal of argumentation available for supporting the newly adopted position.

That is why it has always seemed to me that, in appropriate circumstances, there is nothing wrong—quite the contrary—with argumentation that employs the arguer's full arsenal of weapons, even if that means that he will not necessarily be "liked" as a result.

There are subjects on which each of us is "open to persuasion": Our minds are in equipoise on the question, ready to be tilted one way or the other by a competent arguer. But that is rarely the case with matters that touch us deeply—and these latter are precisely the ones that tend to become the subject of our arguments. We may be prepared to listen with positively judicial impartiality and intelligent disinterest to opposing arguments on whether Richard III murdered the two princes in the Tower, or whether our nephew ought to go to Harvard or Yale (on the unlikely assumption that he can get into either); but we are not nearly so ready to change our mind about some politician we admire (or despise), or some federal policy we strongly favor (or oppose), or the qualities of somebody we love (or hate). Changing a person's mind about such a matter—"hitting him where he lives," as they say—is not usually accomplished, particularly in the opening stages, to the accompaniment of flowers and sweet music. And if our mind is indeed forced to change on such a matter, we are not likely to be especially grateful to the person whose argumentation forced us to change it. The point is a close relative of another that is often put this way: "If someone makes us feel that we are thinking, we love him; but if he really makes us think, we hate him."

A genuine change of mind on a subject important to us, in other words, is often—perhaps usually—accompanied by pain. Do not, then, expect to see real progress on such a front registered by the presence of enthusiasm. Nobody, confronted with a really devastating argument against something in which he has hitherto deeply believed, slaps himself on the thigh and shouts, "By gosh, I never thought of that!" On the contrary, the blow will be resented. Very often it will be sustained in obstinate silence. The ego needs time to marshal its defenses—either to try to restore the toppled idol, or to come to terms with the toppling, or (at the very least) to regain its own shattered composure.

It is precisely then, however—in the silent weeks or months after the argument, when perhaps no one else is present and the defeated arguer confronts only himself and the recollection of his defeat—that the argument may truly be said to be "won." Because then, if ever, is when the loser of the argument will tacitly abandon his former position. He may never admit to having changed his mind at all; but at the very least he will have rearranged his mental furniture, to insure that he does not hereafter sit, so often or so heavily, on that all too demonstrably fragile chair.

That brings us full circle to the point from which we departed: those occasions on which a debater who already has the support of a majority of the target audience, and who needs only to hold onto that support in order to "win," is justified in reinforcing his supporters' enthusiasm at the expense of sacrificing converts who might be lured from the other side by a gentler, less aggressive approach. If the desideratum is to maximize the support immediately available for one's position (as in the case of my debate before the Yale Political Union), then care must be taken not to offend any possible convert. If on the other hand, as was not infrequently my situation on "The Advocates," one feels reasonably confident of winning a vote by a comfortable majority, and can afford to risk alienating wholly intransigent viewers in the hope of permanently changing a number of changeable minds, then a much heavier attack may be justified.

Years ago I participated in an "Advocates" show from Washington on the question, "Should the Government limit the tar and nicotine in cigarettes?" Miller took the affirmative, and I the negative. Not unexpectedly his team offered *inter alia* a gory color film of a tumor the size of a grapefruit being removed from a human lung, and followed that up with a "crawler" (a long list, usually moving up from the bottom of the screen and out the top) showing all the organizations, from the Boy Scouts to the American Medical Association, that had affirmed the dangers of smoking. In response, I offered what I could: the head of a medical committee funded by the tobacco industry to assess the scientific evidence—a learned and thoroughly respectable physician who insisted that the statistical correlations then available (this was January 1971) did not establish a firm link between smoking and lung cancer.

Then I moved on to my strongest ground for opposing the proposed limitation: the libertarian contention that, once people have been adequately informed of the alleged hazards of smoking (as they surely have been by now), they ought to be allowed to go on smoking if they want to—under circumstances, of course, that take into reasonable account the wishes of other people in public places, and always provided that any possible deleterious consequences of their conduct fall only on themselves and not proximately on anyone else, or on society as a whole.

In support of this contention I put on the stand a witness identified simply as "Mr. James Levy, smoker." Levy, a friend of mine in the advertising business, had exactly the quality of nervous, half-humorous latitudinarianism I needed in that slot. He also smoked like the proverbial chimney. Special dispensation was obtained to permit him to smoke on the witness stand—a mercy he would almost surely have required in any case. Wreathed in clouds of smoke, he aptly symbolized the hypothetical individual I wanted the audience to consider: an intelligent man, fully informed of the possible perils, who nevertheless wanted to smoke anyway.

Knowing from previous experience that TV viewers who watched "The Advocates," or at least those who voted on its questions, were very much a live-and-let-live bunch, I was reasonably sure that I would win the vote on the issue, despite Miller's ghastly film. I therefore allowed myself, in cross-examining Miller's chief witness for the proposal, Senator Frank Moss of Utah (who had sponsored the bill to limit tar and nicotine), a slyly *ad hominem* attack that I knew would delight viewers on my side, however much it might annoy the enemies of tobacco.

Moss was a three-term Senate veteran, rather full of himself and very much on his dignity. (He was to be defeated in 1976, in his fourth bid for election, by a youthful conservative Republican, Orrin Hatch.) I inquired mildly whether he didn't think obesity caused by overeating was a far greater menace to public health than smoking, in view of the cardiovascular and other ills associated with it, and whether he would therefore introduce a bill to eliminate the sugar content in our various foods and replace it with saccharin as a means of controlling obesity.* He replied cautiously that he would, if the medical evidence showed sugar to be a danger as great as tobacco. I pressed the point:

RUSHER: "Isn't it a perfectly well known fact in all medical circles that obesity is one of the—probably the—greatest causes of ill health in the United States, and that *this is caused in large part by sugar* (and fats, which we're coming to)?"

MOSS: "Well, I'm not a doctor, but I know there's a lot of concern." Whereupon I got in my little dig.

RUSHER: "It would be very hard, though, on the sugar industry in Utah, wouldn't it, Senator?"

The live audience laughed appreciatively at my point—and so, probably, did the members of the TV audience, for a majority voted against Moss's proposal. Moss, after all (as my teasing remark suggested), wasn't being much of a hero in doing highly visible battle against tobacco. He was a Mormon himself, from the state where Mormonism is dominant and tobacco was anathema long before anybody suspected it might have a connection with lung cancer. Sugar, however, is a Utah crop. (I only wish, in retrospect, that I had asked my researcher to find out whether Moss, in the course of senatorial log-rolling, had won support for Utah agricultural subsidies by voting for the large federal subsidies to the tobacco farmers of North Carolina and elsewhere.)

Shortly after that program, a veteran member of Miller's team came up to me. He was personally liberal in his politics, and had shared the prevailing conviction of the Miller squad that I was simply an avatar of Satan. But, as he explained to me on this occasion, our nicotine show was the first one in which he had found himself, as a sort of left-libertarian, personally on my side of the argument.

* This was before the flap over saccharin.

Evidently he had found the experience highly agreeable, for he concluded by saying, "I've decided that the reason I disliked you on
those other shows was that *you were hurting our side.* And I'm
going to try, hereafter, to be a little more objective about you."

A generous compliment, which underlines my point: Whatever
else effective argumentation may be, it is not reducible to a simple
matter of "being liked." Be coolly polite, by all means (though we
shall have more to say about the large matter of courtesy later on);
but there will be plenty of times when a hard-hitting attack is
justified even though it may irritate a portion of the audience.

WHO HAS THE INITIATIVE?

Normally this will have been decided, at least in formal terms, by
a proper definition of the subject to be argued. As indicated in the
section on that problem, the "affirmative" will ordinarily espouse
that side of the issue that calls for a change in the status quo. And
with the affirmative there will usually go the right (and duty) to
speak first, and the obligation to make the case for the change proposed. In other words, if the target audience, after the argument, is
undecided whether the proposed change is desirable or not, the negative has won: The affirmative must actually persuade in order to
prevail, whereas the negative can prevail either by persuading the audience to its view or by leaving it in a state of equipoise or indeci-
sion.

There will be times, however, when for any one of a number of
reasons the topic has not been precisely enough defined to determine
which adversary has the affirmative. I am writing this on a plane
from San Francisco to Atlanta, whence I shall transfer to one for
Spartanburg, S.C., where I am to speak this evening at Converse College. My speaking agent made the arrangements, and I had not even
realized until recently that the occasion would take the form of a
debate. But the over-all topic of the two-day meeting of which my
speech is to be a part is "Business and Human Values," and I find
that I am one of two principal speakers on this evening's program.
The other is Robert Heilbroner, Norman Thomas Professor of Economics at the New School for Social Research in New York City.

Bob Heilbroner, whom I have debated before, is a noted and able exegete of socialist economics, and it is not hard to infer that the sponsors of this evening's program have a debate of sorts in mind. But what is the topic? "Business and Human Values"? Am I, then, to be for "business," and Bob Heilbroner for "human values"? Anyone who read carefully my comments on "Defining the Issue" will know I am too old a trout to be taken with that misshapen fly—nor, I am sure, do the sponsors expect quite so unfair a division of the labor. More likely they expect a fair amount of genteel disagreement centering around some such unstated but implicit question as, "Does American business adequately serve human values?"—with me taking the affirmative and Heilbroner the negative. In that event there is a case for my going first—but do I really have "the initiative"?

In a more formal context (e.g., before the Cambridge Union) the question might well be phrased, "Resolved: That American business does not adequately serve human values," with Heilbroner in effect attacking the status quo, while I defend it. In that case he would go first, and—more important—would have the initiative. He would have to try to posit certain "human values," defend their intrinsic desirability, establish some sort of obligation on the part of business to serve them, and prove that business is failing to do so. Plenty of room there for counterattack!

Actually, however, the "debate" tonight is clearly going to be much less formal than that. And it is accordingly unclear exactly who has the initiative. Heilbroner will have some prepared remarks, which may (or may not) have much direct bearing on how business serves human values. I perforce have prepared some notes that mention business' alleged insensitivity to certain human values (e.g., motives other than profit), rebut the charge insofar as possible, point out other human values that American business brilliantly serves (widespread prosperity, economic efficiency and responsiveness, and an economic climate wholly compatible with human freedom), and go over to the offensive in a conclusion that alleges that the current criticism of business is actually the cutting edge of an attack by a new class ("public sector" academicians, communicators, and publicists, allegedly speaking for the "public interest") which seeks to topple and replace business as America's dominant social institution.

I shall take a certain amount of care to try to be "liked," since the audience will apparently consist not only of businessmen (my natural allies) and academicians (Bob Heilbroner's) but also of students.

The initiative, in such a situation, is more or less hopelessly and permanently mislaid. It is thus not even clear which of us will speak first. (Alphabetical order? Flip a coin?) A certain price will perforce be paid, in terms of intellectual precision: Our positions may not collide squarely, and a clear-cut decision may thus not be possible. But a certain stimulus and focus will at least have been lent, by the pseudo-debate format, to a discussion that might otherwise ramble uncontrollably (and boringly) all over the immense area signified by the topic, "Business and Human Values."

Where one side or the other does clearly have the initiative, however (and with it, usually, the dubious honor of speaking first), certain advantages and disadvantages follow as the night the day. I have already mentioned one: The side with the initiative has the very considerable burden of proving its point, to the satisfaction of whatever audience, judges, or adversary there may be. The opposition need only keep him from proving it—it need not prove the reverse.

With the burden of proof goes a potential advantage, however. Even when the subject of the argument has been chosen with great precision, the arguer who speaks first can often determine, by what he chooses to discuss (and not discuss), much of the actual shape of the argument. A comical illustration of this was provided by a *New Yorker* cartoon some years ago, in which a drunken and disheveled husband, coming home inexcusably late at night, was confronted at the front door by his furious wife, who brandished a rolling pin in her hand. He raises his hand, and gets in the first words: "Stop! You look beautiful when you're angry."

Similarly, in less domestic contexts, the first speaker can try to narrow or broaden the topic, or at the very least define the tone in which the discussion will take place. I remember a radio talk show during the Vietnam war in which a hawkish young lady of my acquaintance was scheduled to debate a spokeswoman for Women Strike for Peace. Before the program began, the talk-show host ventured a guess (no doubt also a hope) that the program would be a lively one, with the fur flying. "Oh, surely not," purred the lady from

WSP. "How could anybody disagree about peace?" In a sense, of course, she was trying to define the subject; but failing that, she had certainly gone far toward setting the tone.

"I care not who writes a nation's laws," goes the old saying, "as long as I can write its songs." That makes essentially the same point: Tone often dominates substance. It is well-nigh impossible for a debater to sustain a high level of virtuous dudgeon if his opponent is being craftily soothing, or (worse yet) witty. Answering a question in the House of Commons, Winston Churchill once reduced his questioner to sputtering rage. Whereupon the master orator turned avuncular and solicitous: "The honorable gentleman," Churchill counseled genially, "really ought not to generate more indignation than he can conveniently contain." (Which I doubt helped very much— or was intended to!)

As the last paragraph indicates, having the initiative does not by any means *guarantee* the power to set the tone: It merely offers the first opportunity, which is subject to rebuttal in certain circumstances. The drunken husband mentioned earlier almost certainly did not succeed in his brave attempt to deflect his wife from the real issue. And a debater speaking first who sets too light a tone (or deals with the subject too narrowly, omitting matters that cannot sensibly be omitted) is in danger of being attacked by the following speaker very successfully from higher ground.

By and large, therefore, I am inclined to favor speaking second whenever the situation permits. The speaker who goes first must necessarily reveal the basic structure of his case, as well as most of its supporting argumentation. And if he has, as he undeniably does, some chance to set the tone of the argument or even define its subject, these achievements are always subject to modification or outright reversal when the second speaker's turn comes.

I am emphatically *not* saying, however, that a speaker ought to seek to speak second in order to turn his own presentation into little more than a rebuttal of his opponent's points. This fallacious idea appeals to many lazy and insecure arguers, who fondly imagine they are taking sly advantage of their opponent's folly or bad luck in going first. Nothing could be farther from the truth; to borrow Talleyrand's epigram, such a notion is worse than a crime: It is a blunder. The arguer who has no better plan than to rebut his opponent's points is doomed before he begins, for his opponent is bound to score *some* yardage, while he is condemned only to resist, without scoring any of his own.

This is just as true of a debater who has the negative as it is of one upholding the affirmative of a proposition. For upholding the negative is not merely a matter of rebutting points made by the affirmative: There will invariably be subordinate affirmative points buried in the structure of a negative case, and these must be established with precisely the same care and diligence (and by the same techniques) as the affirmative case itself.

The proper time for rebuttal material—i.e., material directly responding to points made by an opponent—is the rebuttal period, specifically set aside late in a debate for that purpose, or (if the argument is not so formally structured) in a comparable period of separately allocated time consciously chosen and so designated by the arguer himself. Even if the first speaker has made a superficially persuasive case, it will usually be better to announce that it will be dealt with later, in the rebuttal period, rather than waste valuable time trying to cope with it during one's own presentation-in-chief.

I am forever amazed at the number of professional speakers who roam American platforms, perhaps especially those on its campuses, insulting their audiences' intelligence (and incidentally ripping off their sponsors) by ignoring even these minimal guidelines to orderly and constructive debate. I remember one speaker in particular, a highly popular fixture of college debates during the later 1960s, who combined sloth and rudeness in a blend all his own. The rudeness came first: He was practically always late, keeping the audience and his opponent waiting for anywhere up to an hour for his blessed advent. Then came the sloth: It invariably turned out that he had not prepared, even casually, for the debate. He was planning to listen to whatever his opponent might say, then use his own time to rebut that, relying on his wits and experience to toss up enough arguments, or at least wisecracks, of one sort or another to give a superficial impression of a case. This strategy naturally required that he go second —a necessity that frequently occasioned more rudeness: i.e., any amount of sneakiness or pressure (not overlooking a blunt appeal for mercy) required to produce the result.

Luckily for him, this gentleman almost always spoke before student audiences heavily predisposed in his favor, so the *net* effect of his performance was usually masked by a standing ovation. But I doubt that he swayed in his favor many minds in the audience capable of even a little discrimination. Certainly from my standpoint, once I had mastered my hostility toward the antagonistic audience, he was a comparatively easy opponent to debate; it wasn't hard to be more courteous, more thoughtful, or better informed than he was.

His example raises, however, the question of just how far it is proper to go in pursuit of that second speaking slot. Of course, if the debate is to be conducted along formal lines, with a properly stated question, it will usually be clear who has the affirmative of the question and who, therefore, goes first. In such a case, my advice is: Do not waste time maneuvering for second place. Accept the normal burden of the affirmative, rather than skew the debate into a false order, and make the most of the first speaker's opportunity to define the topic, or at least the tone, of the discussion.

If the argument is less structured—a business conference, for example, or a family dispute—it may be enough to bide your time and let the natural eagerness of your adversary or adversaries sweep them forward into talking first.

In many arguments of all types, however, there will be occasions when the topic is too muzzy to yield a definable affirmative and negative, and your opponent is too wily to accept the first speaking slot merely because you kindly offer it to him. Worse yet, the sponsor or presiding officer will often have decided the order of speakers on some arbitrary basis—not uncommonly pure bias, by the way. In that case, given the (moderate) importance of the second slot, it may not be inappropriate to suggest that the order of the speakers be determined by flipping a coin. (Alphabetical order is another possibility, unless your own name is closer to Abernathy than Zimmerman.)

WHO HAS THE LAST WORD?

We have saved until last, however, what is perhaps the most important single advantage of speaking second, though technically separable from it: namely, having the last word.

Women, instinctively recognizing the value of the last word, reserved it for themselves, in the days before Women's Lib, as one of the hereditary privileges of their sex. In these more enlightened times that grand old tradition may have fallen into desuetude (though I still seem to detect its presence in many situations). In any case, there are plenty of instances in which no women are participating in the debate, or in which the tradition must give way to more formal rules. In one way or another the question of who goes last is frequently up for decision, and it is almost always worth a fair amount of discreet battling over.

This is especially true where some immediate action is desired as a result of the argument: either action by the adversary or action by a target audience. In "The Advocates," as mentioned earlier, the TV audience was invited to send in its votes on the subject under debate. At the end of nearly an hour of intense confrontation and hot dispute, each advocate was offered sixty seconds in which to sum up. Which one got the coveted last word was almost always a pure byproduct of the form of the question, since under the show's rules the advocate for the negative was awarded it; but that often simply fueled a preliminary argument over the form of the question. To look into the TV camera's eye (which meant, in effect, directly into the eyes of millions of viewers simultaneously) and sum up one's strongest arguments, capping the summation with an appeal for a vote in favor of one's side, was a powerful stimulus to action—and, of course, much more effective if the very next thing the audience heard was the address to which its postcards should be sent, rather than a recapitulation of the best arguments for the *other* side.

In formal debates the right to the last word is theoretically tied rigorously, in one way or another, to such questions as who goes first, whether the rebuttals are in reverse order, whether there are to be summations, etc. These considerations may nevertheless yield a surprising amount of flexibility in this matter of the last word; but there is a separate chapter on tactical considerations in formal debates, and I will defer consideration of this point, in connection with formal debates, until that chapter.

In less formal contexts—panels, for example, or loosely structured debates—a competent arguer will ordinarily and quite properly seek the advantage of the last word unless it would somehow be plainly unfair for him to have it. Often the disadvantage of going first is recognized and counterbalanced by offering the arguer who has accepted it the right to speak last—e.g., in rebuttal or summation. Where there are only two panelists or debaters, however, this may lead to a rather unsatisfactory order: A, B, B, A—thus forcing B to give his rebuttal or summation immediately following his own presentation-in-chief. Sometimes this awkward situation can be alleviated by having questions from the audience, or some other sort of interruption, between B's two statements.

In wholly unstructured arguments, of course—e.g., with a spouse or taxi driver—who has the last word unfortunately tends to be largely a question of who has the leatheriest lungs, or who cares most.

In spending so much time on such collateral matters as who speaks first, who has the last word, etc., I hope I have not left the mistaken impression that these considerations are much more, in relative terms, than simply makeweights. A poor arguer will rarely best a competent one simply because he has managed to gain the advantage of the second speaking slot or the last word, and certainly an intrinsically sound argument will seldom be overcome by an unsound one merely because the latter happens to be stated later, or last.

But we are properly concerned here with every consideration that militates in favor of winning, and between evenly matched adversaries—or in the case of evenly balanced questions—such considerations as the order of speakers unquestionably can make a significant difference. They are well worth the time of any competent arguer.

SHOULD THE NEGATIVE PROPOSE AN ALTERNATIVE?

I have said above that the affirmative in a typical debate, or even in a more loosely structured argument, has the burden of proving its case; the negative need not disprove it, or prove the desirability of some alternative. This is the general rule, and is well illustrated by the loosely correct proposition that a person being prosecuted for a crime is deemed innocent until proved guilty. Proof of guilt is up to the prosecution; the defendant need not prove that some other specific person committed the crime.

Nevertheless, there are undeniably occasions when it is desirable for the negative to offer some alternative proposal, whether it is technically obliged to do so or not. The situation just discussed is one example: Obviously, the lawyer for a man on trial for murder will demonstrate, if he can, that somebody else committed the murder. The best defense is often a strong offense, just as the saying goes.

As already mentioned, I recently agreed to debate former U.S. Senator Eugene McCarthy on the formal question, "Is conservatism the best course for America in the 1980s?" I accepted this rather lopsided formulation of the issue because Gene was reluctant to be locked into arguing that liberalism (at least in some of its present definitions) was a preferable course. Nevertheless, I felt that I was within bounds in suggesting to our college audience that Senator McCarthy ought to propose *some* alternative course, since by definition he didn't agree with mine. "You can't beat somebody with nobody," I pointed out, quoting the oldest adage in politics, "and similarly you can't beat something with nothing."

Senator McCarthy apparently agreed, for he proceeded to offer some proposals of his own, and the debate eventually seemed to turn in large part on whether the audience felt the negative had, in this case, at least discharged its implicit burden of demonstrating that mine was not the only conceivable course for America in the 1980s.

A more dryly technical—and, I thought, less successful—approach to the obligations of the negative was taken by Carl Oglesby, one of the early national leaders of Students for a Democratic Society (SDS), in a debate with me at Virginia Polytechnic Institute in the early 1960s. I have forgotten the precise question we were debating, or even who technically had the affirmative, but I remember distinctly that Oglesby, to my astonishment and delight, made a brilliant attack on the Leviathan state and the general perniciousness of Big Government. (I had not yet learned that early on in the 1960s the burgeoning New Left was, on left-libertarian principles, as opposed to these evils as we conservatives were.)

I was about to rise and nominate Oglesby for the Presidency when some warning light in my skull flashed on briefly and prompted me to inquire, preliminarily, exactly what alternative to Big Government Oglesby had in mind. He had made a savage and triumphant attack upon it, but this seemed to me another of those instances in which the negative was, if not theoretically, then at least tonally, obliged to go one step further and propose an alternative. As a conservative I felt there were certainly alternatives available, but I wanted to hear Oglesby's.

He surprised me again, and this time disappointed me, by replying that it wasn't up to him to propose an alternative. True enough, in theory; yet his response was somehow unsatisfying. Later on in that hairy decade of the 1960s I decided on the basis of many further debates with New Leftists—most of them far less coherent and articulate than Oglesby, who seemed to fall by the wayside—that their inability (or unwillingness) to propose an alternative to the hated "System" they were so good at condemning was an important limitation on their rhetorical effectiveness.

To sum up the point, the negative's technical privilege of confining itself to demolishing the affirmative's proposal without offering one of its own must be exercised with discretion. If the question under discussion is a proposed change in the status quo, it may well be sufficient to attack the proposed change and merely defend the status quo. But *in attacking the status quo* a competent arguer will usually take care to equip himself with a plausible alternative, and in any debate touching on the future a debater will be well advised to have a plan for it, even if his plan is only a more or less featureless extension of the status quo.

I have discussed this problem, and some of its predecessors, in terms suitable for a semiformal debate, but the same rules apply to a panel discussion, a business conference, or a domestic argument. A proposed business merger can sometimes be attacked solely on its own manifest demerits, but it will often be advisable to show how the desired expansion can be achieved in another way or by merger with a different company. A wife's suggestion of a European holiday can (perhaps) be opposed successfully purely on grounds of expense, but an alternative proposal (Florida or Mexico or Hawaii) can often pave the way for at least relative frugality. (Of course, she may have planned it that way all along!)

Whatever the technical form or level of the argument then, the above are some strategic and tactical considerations that ought to be confronted at the outset. We know now what is up for discussion, what our basic objective in this particular argument is, and (subject to various modifications) who has the ball. There remains, however, one other important subject that must be considered at the very outset, and that is the adversary: not the adversary as a Platonic form, but *this adversary himself, in particular*. What do we know about him?

SIZING UP THE OPPOSITION

Since it takes two to argue, and no two opponents are ever exactly alike (in fact, not even the same opponent is ever exactly the same on the next go-around), one important factor to be considered at the outset of any argument is the precise nature of the opponent: his general attitude, his strengths and weaknesses, his mood, and much else. This is equally true whether the opponent is one's brother-in-law or one's employer or a rival debater before the Cambridge Union.

Take the matter of general attitude. More than once I have approached a debate with a total—and near fatal—misconception of my opponent's basic attitude toward it and toward me. A good many years ago a college professor persuaded one of the New York-area radio stations to let him use its facilities to do a pilot show for what he (and presumably the station) hoped might become a continuing program in a debate format. The professor was kind enough to want me to be one of the two protagonists for the pilot show, and couched his invitation in terms flattering enough to win my assent. I was particularly delighted to hear that my opponent would be the noted radio comedian, Henry Morgan.

I had listened to Morgan years before, when he had his own program, and he was one of my favorite radio comics. ("Who," he was asked in a skit based on "The Answer Man," "are the chief users of goat's milk?"—to which he promptly responded, with Olympian authority, "Goats.") I was not terribly surprised to learn that Morgan was, politically speaking, liberal enough to agree to debate me on the professor's pilot show, nor did I care; I looked forward to meeting him at long last.

The encounter took place in one of those gloomy sound studios in mid-Manhattan, replete with directional mikes and minimal furniture. On being introduced, I told Morgan effusively how much I had enjoyed listening to him. He responded noncommittally, with a sort of let's-get-on-with-it air, and get on with it we did.

It swiftly transpired that getting his hands, figuratively speaking, around my throat was one of Henry Morgan's highest ambitions. Presumably he had heard me on one or more of those late-night talk shows so popular on New York radio in the early 1960s—Long John Nebel, or Barry Farber—and found my views or their presentation, or simply me, unendurable. At any rate, he fell on me with the ferocity of a Kodiak bear who hadn't eaten in months. I bicycled furiously backward while mastering my astonishment, and ultimately managed to counterattack on his frequency, so to speak. In fact, the pilot show eventually got so bloody that the professor not surprisingly failed to sell the station the concept of a program modeled on it.

But the point, for our present purposes, is that I was quite mistaken to assume, as I had, that merely because I liked Morgan, Morgan would like me.

Much the same thing happened years later when "The Advocates" agreed to put on a sort of miniature version of one of its programs as a part of the "Dick Cavett Show." I was introduced to Cavett briefly at his office a day or two before the show. I had seen him on TV, of course, but had no particular sentiment concerning him one way or the other. He, however, gave early indication of having had a noseful of Rusher: His first words when we shook hands were, "Are you *always* on the 'Barry Farber Show,' or only when I'm listening?" I naively took this, however, merely as a graceful compliment to my ubiquity—and was accordingly flabbergasted when on the night of the show, appearing as a "witness" for the other side, Cavett responded to my cross-examination with a barrage of sarcastic remarks aimed at me personally. Reacting automatically (but correctly), I just stood aside and let Cavett thunder by, rather like a bull missing the toreador. The reaction of the TV audience to Cavett's attack, interestingly enough, was so negative that I was promptly asked to appear on his show again, this time on my own, to be treated a bit more kindly!

To be entirely fair, I am sure many liberals could tell similar stories about their encounters with me. Most of my adversaries, after all, have been men and women long experienced in debate and accustomed to sparring with adversaries who believe (as they themselves do) that the future scarcely hinges on this particular encounter. I, on the other hand, have frequently psyched myself into believing that the entire future did in fact hinge on this particular encounter, and that my opponent was, consciously or otherwise, the instrument of Satan. The resulting onslaught must have made more than one accomplished debater wonder what he had climbed into the ring with.

I remember with special remorse a contest on Barry Farber's radio talk show with Professor (later Dean) Robert McKay of NYU Law School. The debate was over some typical liberal-conservative dispute in the field of civil liberties, and McKay, as far as I was concerned at the time, was just one more designing leftist standing between America and salvation. I behaved—or rather misbehaved—accordingly. I don't know what McKay thought of my performance (I do remember that his response was characteristically mild); perhaps it left no permanent impression on him, despite my best—or worst—efforts. In any case, however, our acquaintance survived that early encounter and ripened, during the years we served together on the National News Council, into a warm friendship. Bob McKay and I still do not always agree, but I know him to be one of the gentlest, most judicious, and just generally *nicest* people I have ever met. He, in turn, was magnanimous enough to arrange for me to receive in 1973 the "Distinguished Citizen Award" of NYU Law School for my "able articulation of the conservative viewpoint."

Remember, then, to pay attention to your opponent's general attitude—toward the subject and toward you personally. Toward the subject: Is he passionately concerned, or actually rather indifferent?

Toward you: Is he an old and implacable foe, a friend merely needing guidance, or a thoroughly professional adversary?

Second, what are your adversary's particular strengths and weaknesses? One of the most dangerous of all dilemmas for a competent arguer is to find himself forced to tangle with a renowned expert squarely in the field of the latter's acknowledged expertise.

Some years ago a *National Review* subscriber out in Colorado wrote to say that his hobby was breeding racing greyhounds, and that he had, in a burst of enthusiasm for his favorite magazine, named one entire litter after NR's leading personalities: Bill Buckley, Bill Rusher, James Burnham, Russell Kirk, Frank Meyer, and Priscilla Buckley. He added that Bill Buckley (the dog, that is), on being entered at the track in Denver, had attracted considerably more money in wagers than was justified strictly by his record—the reward of fame, obviously.

I inquired about the dog named Bill Rusher. This animal, it turned out, shared the general greyhound trait of fighting with others of his kind—which is why greyhounds are usually muzzled. Bill Rusher, however, had a bad habit of getting into fights with the other greyhounds when he had his muzzle on and they didn't. "He just doesn't think," said his owner.

Never make my canine namesake's mistake!

Sometimes, of course, you may find yourself in a situation where you are forced to argue with somebody who is notoriously better informed on the subject at hand than you are. My entire education in economics consisted of a single two-semester course at Princeton. Yet on "The Advocates" I was, at one time or another, required to cross-examine on that complex subject John Kenneth Galbraith, Walter Heller (former chairman of the Council of Economic Advisers), and Nobel Prize-winner Paul Samuelson.

As a matter of fact, being a "regular" advocate on that program more often than not required me to take on, in cross-examination, justly famous experts in all sorts of fields concerning which, in the very nature of things, I was able to acquire only the most rudimentary orientation. I would often have to prepare to cross swords on, say, agribusiness with a senator from a farm state, then the very next night debate the professionalizing of the Olympics with a Gold

Medal winner. It was a bit like requiring a tiger to get in a tank and battle a series of sharks: He had the benefit of experience, but water was their home environment. In sheer self-defense, I learned a lot about swimming.

A later section of this book will discuss how best to cope with towering experts. Meanwhile, suffice it to say that a competent arguer will take careful note of his adversary's strengths and try to avoid bringing these into play.

How about his weaknesses? How far is it proper to take advantage of those? Here we approach the domain of ethics, and I might as well say at the outset that the question is often not an easy one to answer.

Since the object of arguing is usually to prevail, in one sense or another, and since one perfectly proper way to prevail is to deploy a superior array of facts to support one's position, it seems clear that the expert, at least, cannot be accused of hitting below the belt merely because he relies successfully on his expertise. If he is indeed "taking advantage of his opponent's weakness," it is a weakness (inferior factual information) that his opponent simply had no business having. The only danger the expert must guard against is overwhelming his opponent so spectacularly that the target audience (if there is one) finds its sympathies swinging toward the latter. For this reason, expertise ought ordinarily to be deployed with a becoming modesty.

But what about the arguer whose superiority to his opponent consists, not of a larger supply of factual information, but of a more impressive and authoritative bearing (for example), or of intellectual quickness, or of a more winning personality—in short, of personal characteristics, innate or acquired, that count in his favor? Plenty of people are convinced that they lost some argument which by rights they ought to have won, simply because their opponent "was so glib." And they nurse a sense of injustice.

If there is injustice here, however (and there probably is), it derives from an inequality imposed upon the protagonists at birth, or in childhood. It cannot be blamed on the abler individual, and he ought not to be criticized, any more than the expert, for employing the advantage it gives him. "It is as easy for the strong man to be strong as it is for the weak to be weak," and I think this Emersonian dictum can be reformulated with equal accuracy: "It is as hard for the strong man to be weak as it is for the weak to be strong."

As recounted earlier, Bill Buckley once told me, with that candor one often displays to a new friend, "I don't think I have an exceptionally powerful mind, but I do think I have an exceptionally quick one." When challenged and on the *qui vive*, Buckley can assess an opponent's statement, formulate his reply, decorate it with a stinging witticism, deliver it, and be on the other side of town, so to speak, launching a counterattack on some quite different sector of the front, before his opponent has understood, let alone refuted, Bill's response to his first point. I have myself been the victim of those Stonewall Jackson cavalry tactics on Bill's part too often to doubt that his intellectual speed and agility, quite apart from whatever intrinsic merit his argument on a given point may have, are a formidable advantage.

But are they an *unfair* advantage? I have often wished I could think so, but I can't. We are not all equally endowed in every respect. People will pay cash to listen to Bill's friend Fernando Valenti play Mozart's Twelve Variations on the harpsichord, while Buckley's more laborious version, played for the assembled guests at Bohemian Grove in the summer of 1978, brought forth only an anguished cry from one listener: "Vote No on Variation Thirteen!"

As in the case of an expert, the arguer exceptionally well endowed with useful personal characteristics is well advised not to throw his weight around too recklessly. There is something in all of us that dislikes an obvious winner, and at least one Greek finally tired of hearing Aristedes called "the Just." But it was hardly unfair of Aristedes to let his reputation as a just man add weight to the positions he took on given issues.

Thus far, the reader will have noted, I have tended to favor letting the stronger arguer (whether stronger by virtue of his expertise or of superior personal characteristics) exploit his advantage over a weaker opponent. But there are situations where it might be unethical to do so. Take, for example, the situation where one arguer happens to know (and his adversary does not) some basic fact greatly helpful to that adversary's case. Is the possessor of the information duty-bound

to reveal it, even though his case will be severely damaged by the rev-
elation?

Let's be entirely frank. Many people wouldn't dream of disclosing
such information and, more important, wouldn't consider themselves
ethically bound to do so. ("The other guy can take care of himself,
can't he? If not, that's his tough luck.") Though no example from
my own experience comes readily to mind, I have no doubt that I
myself have more than once withheld some tidbit that an adversary
would have been grateful to have.

But I'm afraid the best practice condemns that sort of thing, at
least where the withheld fact is highly material—i.e., not just a make-
weight but potentially an important factor in the over-all balance of
the argumentation. The rule in criminal prosecutions (although, like
other rules, sometimes honored in the breach) is especially clear: A
prosecutor who comes into possession of evidence important to the
defendant's case is ethically bound to disclose it, even if it hurts his
own. This would certainly be true of a prosecutor who, midway
through a criminal trial, came across documentary evidence proving
the defendant innocent: If he suppressed the evidence and was later
caught, contempt of court (let alone reversal) would be one possible
penalty. The reverse situation—i.e., one in which a defense attorney
discovers irrefutable evidence of the defendant's guilt—is probably
commoner, and no doubt such evidence is often suppressed, whatever the ethical imperatives may be. But the rule, at least technically,
remains the same: The attorney is *theoretically* obliged to turn over
the evidence, and modify his defense accordingly (e.g., by pleading
insanity, rather than sticking to an alibi defense that the new evidence has demolished).

To be sure, the obligation of an attorney is somewhat heavier than
that of many an advocate in a less formal proceeding because every
attorney is, at least in theory, an "officer of the court," as committed
as the judge himself to the search for the ultimate truth of whatever
matter is at issue. But the underlying analysis is the same whether
the arguer is an attorney pressing an appeal before the U. S. Supreme
Court, or a partner participating in a discussion over which of several
courses a business ought to adopt, or a husband haggling with his
wife over which school their son ought to attend. The proper remedy

for a newly discovered fact that aids one's adversary is *not* to conceal it, but to divulge it and revise one's own position and argumentation to take it into account.

Pure misconduct of one sort or another—e.g., fabricating evidence—won't be discussed here because it simply has no place in an honorably conducted argument. Any argument that needs that kind of support ought never to have been embarked on in the first place.

So much, then, for the preparatory stages of an argument. The question has now been defined, and the format chosen. The purpose of the argument, and the strengths and weaknesses of the adversary, have been carefully considered. So "Cry havoc, and let slip the dogs of war!"

We are at last ready to begin the argument.

VIII

TECHNIQUES OF
ARGUMENTATION

To win an argument—i.e., to make an unassailable case for a given
proposition—the arguer must ordinarily either (1) demonstrate that
the proposition follows from the application of some relevant *principle*, or (2) demonstrate that it follows from the marshaling of relevant *facts*, or (3) do both.

A *principle* is an argument that is derived from the general experience of the race and has been enshrined in some permanent form:
Honesty is the best policy. Thou shalt not kill. Never drink till the
sun is over the yardarm. In theory, a principle governs any situation
to which it is applicable. It can be attacked directly (e.g., by arguing
that honesty is *not* the best policy), but as that illustration demonstrates, a recognized principle usually contains enough truth to make
that course inadvisable. Attacks on a principle, therefore, more com-
monly involve its relevance ("Honesty is indeed the best policy, but
I am not suggesting anything dishonest").

A *fact*, for purposes of argumentation, is any factual statement
that tends to favor the proposition being argued: either because it
offers a favorable analogy or points to a desired consequence, or because in some other way it assists the proposition. If a man wants to
persuade his wife that they should spend Sunday afternoon visiting
his Aunt Lulu, relevant facts might include: the fact that his wife
enjoyed last month's visit to Aunt Lulu; the associated facts that
Aunt Lulu is wealthy, in poor health, and about to draw up her will;
the fact that it's a nice day for a drive; etc. Countering a factual argument is likewise ordinarily done either directly ("On the contrary,

that last trip gave me a splitting headache") or by assailing its relevance ("Aunt Lulu has already announced she's leaving everything to her daughters"). Whereas a relevant principle will often suffice to win an argument all by itself unless it is successfully countered, facts must often be accumulated and marshaled until they clearly outweigh the countervailing facts adduced by the other side.

Of course, the art of argumentation has been analyzed by others far more deeply than in this quick survey of the use of principles and facts, and subdivisions and variations of the basic techniques have been isolated and given special names (often in Latin—we have a great deal to thank the Jesuits for). But the average person will rarely have the need, and almost never the time, to study the art of argumentation to such depths. Mastery of the basics is what he or she needs, and *principles* and *facts* are the basics.

Naturally, most arguments above the Aunt Lulu level involve a more complex array of both principles and facts, and each side in a major argument will ordinarily have counters, effective to a greater or lesser degree, to the principles and facts adduced by the other. That is why so many important arguments end in a virtual tie, while in others one side prevails only narrowly, or neutral observers disagree as to which has won. We will inspect a few historic arguments to illustrate how first principles, then facts, were adduced by both sides.

THE APPEAL TO PRINCIPLE

Consider the great "isolationist" vs. "interventionist" controversy that wracked America in 1940 and 1941. Few issues since the Civil War have divided Americans more deeply or more passionately. On one side were those (called "isolationists") who regarded the war then under way in Europe as just another in the long series of parochial squabbles that had characterized European history since its dawn. These people believed profoundly that the war was none of America's business, and that it was in our highest interest to stay out of it, however much we might sympathize with England and/or detest Hitler.

On the other side were those who considered that the fascist challenge was the climax of the twentieth century's long struggle with to-

talitarianism, and that the United States neither could nor should re-
frain from ranging itself with Britain in its lonely struggle. Both sides
in the controversy were perfectly sincere, both had impressive arguments on their side, and both believed deeply in the essential virtue
of their case. Moreover, a tremendous amount—including, very
probably, the outcome of the war—plainly hung on who won this
quarrel over American participation.*

Interestingly enough, the argument was by no means easy to
define in liberal vs. conservative terms. A case can be made that isolationism was the traditional position of conservatives in the field of
foreign affairs (though an equally plausible case can be made for regarding the highly "interventionist" concept of Manifest Destiny as
the true conservative position on foreign affairs, or at least a respectable rival for the title). But whatever the situation may have been
prior to 1940, the events of that year—the collapse of France and the
Battle of Britain—brought many conservatives to the conclusion that
Hitler had to be stopped, by American armed intervention if necessary. Most liberals agreed, but by no means all: The Socialist Party
U.S.A., under the leadership of Norman Thomas, was militantly isolationist, regarding the war as merely a brawl between rival British
and German imperialisms. I remember attending, as a heckler, an
America First rally (America First was the umbrella organization of
the isolationists) at Princeton in February 1941. Norman Thomas
(Princeton '05) shared the platform with the isolationist Republican senator from North Dakota, Gerald P. Nye, and solemnly
insisted that the United States could well afford to let not only
Europe but southern South America fall to the Nazis, drawing our
defensive line at "the bulge of Brazil."

The isolationist-interventionist debate of 1940–41 is a useful example of the genre, because it took substantially all of the forms an argument can. It is recent enough to be intelligible, yet remote enough
(or at least so I hope) to be used illustratively without undue risk of
entangling the reader in misunderstandings attributable to his own
predilections on the subject.

---

* I personally was a very young and very passionate "interventionist"; but—as
throughout this book—I have tried not to let my own position intrude on the discussion, other than illustratively.

To the isolationist of 1940, the great principle at stake in the controversy was best stated in what was undoubtedly the single most frequently used quotation of all, from George Washington's Farewell Address to the nation: "Europe has a set of primary interests which to us have none or a very remote relation. . . . It is our true policy to steer clear of permanent alliances with any portion of the foreign world."

The interventionists, for their part, nailed their banner to the mast of freedom: Nazi Germany and its allies represented totalitarianism in its crudest and most menacing (because most aggressive) form. Being denied the imposing, almost awesome authority of Washington as their spokesman, the interventionists looked to the eloquent contemporary leader of Great Britain: Winston Churchill. Churchill, who was himself half American, understood very well the great debate then raging in the United States—and understood also its momentous consequences for Britain. Again and again in speeches aimed directly at American opinion, he pounded home the theme of freedom, and Britain as its defender, and the United States as Britain's ally in that defense. From a score of examples, I offer this one—from his broadcast address on June 16, 1941, accepting by short-wave radio an honorary degree from Rochester University (New York). There has never been a more eloquent appeal for action in the name of the pure principle of freedom:

"Strong tides of emotion, fierce surges of passion, sweep the broad expanses of the Union in this year of fate. In that prodigious travail there are many elemental forces, there is much heart-searching and self-questioning; some pangs, some sorrow, some conflict of voices, but no fear. The world is witnessing the birth throes of a sublime resolve. I shall presume to confess to you that I have no doubts what that resolve will be.

"The destiny of mankind is not decided by material computation. When great causes are on the move in the world, stirring all men's souls, drawing them from their firesides, casting aside comfort, wealth, and the pursuit of happiness in response to impulses at once awe-striking and irresistible, we learn that we are spirits, not animals, and that something is going on in space and time, and beyond space and time, which, whether we like it or not, spells duty.

"A wonderful story is unfolding before our eyes. How it will end we are not allowed to know. But on both sides of the Atlantic we all feel, I repeat, all, that we are a part of it, that our future and that of many generations is at stake. We are sure that the character of human society will be shaped by the resolves we take and the deeds we do. We need not bewail the fact that we have been called upon to face such solemn responsibilities. We may be proud, and even rejoice among our tribulations, that we have been born at this cardinal time for so great an age and so splendid an opportunity of service here below.

"Wickedness, enormous, panoplied, embattled, seemingly triumphant, casts its shadow over Europe and Asia. Laws, customs, and traditions are broken up. Justice is cast from her seat. The rights of the weak are trampled down. The grand freedoms of which the President of the United States has spoken so movingly are spurned and chained. The whole stature of man, his genius, his initiative, and his nobility, is ground down under systems of mechanical barbarism and of organized and scheduled terror.

"For more than a year we British have stood alone, uplifted by your sympathy and respect and sustained by our own unconquerable will-power and by the increasing growth and hopes of your massive aid. In these British islands that look so small upon the map we stand, the faithful guardians of the rights and dearest hopes of a dozen States and nations now gripped and tormented in a base and cruel servitude. Whatever happens we shall endure to the end.

"But what is the explanation of the enslavement of Europe by the German Nazi regime? How did they do it? It is but a few years ago since one united gesture by the peoples, great and small, who are now broken in the dust, would have warded off from mankind the fearful ordeal it has had to undergo. But there was no unity. There was no vision. The nations were pulled down one by one while the others gaped and chattered. One by one, each in his turn, they let themselves be caught. One after another they were felled by brutal violence or poisoned from within by subtle intrigue.

"And now the old lion with her lion cubs at her side stands alone against hunters who are armed with deadly weapons and impelled by desperate and destructive rage. Is the tragedy to repeat itself once more? Ah no! This is not the end of the tale. The stars in their courses proclaim the deliverance of mankind. Not so easily shall the onward progress of the peoples be barred. Not so easily shall the lights of freedom die.

"But time is short. Every month that passes adds to the length and to the perils of the journey that will have to be made. United we stand. Divided we fall. Divided, the dark age returns. United, we can save and guide the world."

Washington versus Churchill! This was heady stuff. Rival principles collided head on. How did the two sides respond?

The counter to the invocation of a principle—any principle—in the course of an argument ordinarily takes one of two basic forms: One either attacks the validity of the principle itself or attacks the propriety of its application to the particular situation.

Both sides in 1940–41 tended to adopt the latter tactic. The interventionists, responding to Washington's famous dictum, argued that what was unquestionably true in the eighteenth century, when the swiftest packet boats took three or four weeks to make the Atlantic crossing, was simply inapplicable in the twentieth, when planes could make the same journey in a matter of hours. The isolationists for their part did not deny the sanctity of freedom as a principle to be defended, but denied that it was authentically at issue in this particular war. Nazi Germany and its allies were undoubtedly obnoxious totalitarian regimes, but the British record, in India and elsewhere, was hardly without stain on the score of human rights; and anyway, what was the Soviet Union doing, fighting on the "side of freedom"? Surely there was a massive anomaly here!

How one came down on the issue of isolationism versus interventionism therefore depended, as far as invocations of principle were concerned, very largely on how one responded to these various contentions. Times had undoubtedly changed since Washington wrote his Farewell Address, but had they rendered its quoted point wholly nugatory? The presence of the Soviet Union on the "side of freedom" in World War II was indeed a major anomaly; but was it a mere accident of history, or did it fatally compromise the cause of freedom?

The attack on a principle (or its application) in an argument may take other and somewhat different forms. For example, even a principle that cannot be disputed, and whose application to the set of facts in question cannot be denied, may be countered by a successful appeal to a principle that is (assertedly) higher still. This was the fundamental strategy of Senator Joseph McCarthy's critics in their familiar statement, "I agree with McCarthy's objectives, but I disapprove of his methods." They were saying, in effect, that it was undoubtedly important to identify and remove secret Communists from positions of influence in our society, and especially in the government, but that McCarthy's techniques in doing so violated even higher principles: the right to hold unorthodox opinions; loyalty to friends; academic freedom, etc. To trample such values in a hunt for hidden Communists, they argued, was to throw out the baby with the bath water.

McCarthy's supporters, incidentally, would usually reply to this array of allegedly transcendent values by arguing that the first was indeed a higher value, but was in this instance being misapplied (the Communists in question were not asserting unorthodox opinions under the protection of the First Amendment but were trying to conceal them—arguably a quite different thing); the second was not in fact transcendent (one's loyalty to one's friends ought not, at least necessarily, to supersede one's obligation to one's country); and the third was simply inapplicable (academic freedom presumably protects the right to assert one's views, not the right to dissimulate them).

THE PLANTED AXIOM

Quite often in an argument one will sense the unasserted presence, in an opponent's argumentation, of a principle or fact he has not openly proclaimed as one on which he is relying but which in fact is an essential part of his case. Sometimes the omission is deliberate: for example, if the adversary hopes the principle will be accepted tacitly, without putting him to the task of defending it openly, or that the unasserted fact will be similarly accepted as axiomatic—i.e., not needing proof. More often, though, he regards the principle as so obvious, or the fact as so clearly axiomatic, that he assumes everyone will take it for granted. Finally, now and then an amateur arguer may sincerely be unaware himself that the unstated principle or fact is a key point in his case.

Whatever the reason for not stating it may be, the other side's interest is usually to identify such a "planted axiom" and drag it out into the light of day, where it can be inspected for validity and applicability. An obvious domestic example might be the wife's question, "What time shall we start for my mother's house next Sunday?" Here the planted axiom is that they will in any case visit her mother's house on Sunday—as (perhaps) they do every Sunday. The only question open for discussion is *when* on Sunday the visit will take place. But the planted axiom is, of course, available for inspection and evaluation; perhaps the husband wants to go to the zoo this Sunday instead. In the interests of diplomacy he may well take care to be a bit gentle in how he goes about exposing and undermining this particular axiom, but in essence that is what he must do.

One splendid example of a planted axiom, drawn from my own experience as a longtime opponent of American recognition of the People's Republic of China, was the assertion of advocates of recognition that it was the height of absurdity for the United States to go on recognizing the Taipei regime as "the Government of China" when in reality its *de facto* control extended only to the island of Taiwan.

The planted axiom here was the proposition that the United States did in fact recognize the Taipei regime as "the Government of China." This would have been palpably absurd if true, but it was simply not true.

It was true that the Taipei regime styled itself as the government of "the Republic of China," and that juridically it was, indisputably, the same government that had once exercised *de facto* control over most of China, until driven by its Communist foes in the civil war to retreat to the island province of Taiwan. But the United States, in the years following Chiang's loss of the mainland in 1949, had carefully distanced itself from the juridical claims of the Taiwan regime.

As a matter of fact, the United States prevented Taipei from signing the 1952 peace treaty with Japan on behalf of China precisely because we did not consider that it was capable of acting "on behalf of

China." And all of the fifty-eight treaties and other agreements signed between Taipei and Washington after 1949 carefully indicate our understanding that Taipei spoke only for those areas under its *de facto* control: Taiwan, the Pescadores, Quemoy, and the Matsus.

Yet so deep was the axiom planted, that America recognized the Taipei regime as "the Government of China," and so diligently was it cultivated, that friend and foe alike came to believe it—regarding it as an anomaly, either excusable or inexcusable depending on one's politics, but in any event most certainly as an anomaly.

Related to this was another axiom, sometimes asserted but often merely planted, to the effect that the United States could ill afford to go on "ignoring 800 million people"—i.e., the mainland Chinese. This implied the (surely debatable) proposition that refusing to recognize a particular regime in Peking—a regime, moreover, given to convulsive and homicidal internal struggles, and exercising a highly uneven influence over events in remote provinces—was the equivalent of ignoring the existence, and even the best interests, of the 800 million Chinese on the mainland. Such casual elisions, however, are a commonplace of debaters' tactics. The point is, be on the lookout for them.

COUNTERING THE APPEAL TO PRINCIPLE

On the other hand, a principle may be openly proclaimed, altogether unassailable, and clearly applicable to one subordinate aspect of a problem, but not so clearly applicable to other aspects of it, or to the problem as a whole, or to the problem *now* (as distinguished from some other time). From my days as a practicing lawyer I remember one lengthy and expensive arbitration that could have been avoided altogether if either party to a franchise agreement for the production of nylon fibers had realized that the long market dominance of the finer grades of nylon thread, used to produce silk stockings, was about to end and yield pride of position to the coarser grades, used in manufacturing airplane tires. In this case, of course, the shift was actually in a factual substratum (viz., which grades of nylon were economically the most important), but both sides had erected a veritable principle of conduct on the prevailing factual situation. When that changed, a principle perfectly valid in the past became quite inapplicable to the present and future.

Or take a hypothetical situation, in which a principle valid in one place may not be so clearly valid in another. I can well imagine that many a multinational corporation that insists on absolute honesty in its domestic American transactions finds itself in a dilemma when it begins doing business abroad. If it is competing against (say) European manufacturers for an important market in a Third World nation, and it becomes plain that the local *mores* absolutely require discreet bribes to government officials in that Third World nation, to grease the way to a deal, and the European competitors are able and willing to give such bribes, what is the American company to do?— adhere to its general principle or treat overseas contracts as a special sub-category of transactions governed by different rules? Note that not only corporate profits, but thousands of American jobs, may hinge on the answer to this by no means easy question.

At times it may be possible to spoil the effect of an adversary's invocation of a principle by arguing that its application in the particular situation under discussion will not yield the result the adversary desires. This was the fundamental—and ultimately successful—argument against Prohibition. The case for Prohibition was firmly grounded on the moral principle that the consumption of alcohol was evil *per se*. Whatever one thought of the principle, very soon the results of Prohibition became apparent, and they raised serious questions as to how well the principle was being served by its application. Instead of becoming a quietly abstemious nation, America developed a whole subculture of speakeasies, rumrunners, and their associated mobsters. Of course, *predicting* such an outcome of Prohibition would have been far more difficult and less convincing than merely noting it when it occurred, but unquestionably the observed consequences of Prohibition were a deadly argument against its continuation.

Another famous way of attacking a principle is to subject it to the technique known as the *reductio ad absurdum*—i.e., apply it to extreme cases, which often reveal intrinsic flaws in the principle, or at least demonstrate significant limitations on its applicability. In practice, the latter is a far commoner effect than the former.

Once on "The Advocates" I was cross-examining a witness who opposed the death penalty in all circumstances. One familiar argument against the death penalty is that even the worst offender may subsequently undergo a miraculous rehabilitation, and executing anyone eliminates that possibility. On the other side of the question, advocates of capital punishment frequently make a point of arguing that it is at least justified in the case of a prisoner already under a life sentence, who thereupon kills another inmate or a guard. Such a person may well reason that if there is no death penalty, he has "nothing left to lose," since he can only receive further consecutive life sentences: He has, in effect, a "license to kill."

The witness I was questioning had made the first of these points on his direct examination, citing the well-known case of a killer who, in prison, took to raising canaries and ultimately became an acknowledged authority on the subject, even to the extent of writing a book about it. This prisoner, however, to whom the press gave the title of "Bird Man of Alcatraz," was not a terribly felicitous example because while in prison he had killed another inmate—thus underscoring one of the arguments for my side. I decided to stress this on cross-examination, pressing the point that if the Bird Man had chosen to kill yet again, there was precious little anybody could do about it:

RUSHER: . . . "What would you have done? Taken away his birds?"

This was a rough and ready sort of *reductio ad absurdum*: To the witness' contention that a life sentence was punishment enough, and that a life prisoner could be adequately deterred from killing again, I responded by suggesting that, in the case of the Bird Man, the only sanction remaining available to the authorities was a slightly ridiculous one. The witness might try—indeed, did try—to counter this with a sober suggestion that other, more effective deterrents might still be available; but the touch of black humor in the *reductio ad absurdum* drove my point home far more forcibly than any merely rational response he might make.

To sum up, then: Invoking a principle in support of your case can assist it mightily because a principle invites assent without putting you to the trouble of proving whatever subject matter it covers. If freedom must be defended everywhere at all costs; if human life is absolutely sacred and never to be taken under any circumstances; if drinking is an evil to be prohibited whatever the consequences; if Communism is to be rooted out of American life regardless of the price we must pay in civil liberties surrendered; if one must invariably visit one's mother-in-law on Sunday; if a corporation must avoid bribery everywhere and all the time—if any one of these propositions is unqualifiedly true, then large areas of otherwise debatable territory are placed beyond discussion.

A principle thus posited may be attacked either directly (human life is in general a good, but not necessarily the highest good) or acknowledged as basically valid but denied applicability in this case— either because a still higher principle governs this case, or because the principle is improperly applied to these particular facts, or because the principle governs only one subdivision of the case, or because its application in these particular circumstances yields undesirable results.

As a practical proposition in debating, you will rarely if ever come across a principle that wholly forecloses argument. There are many such—e.g., the preferability of honorable peace to war—but such principles are rarely seen in the arena of debate because their universal acceptance prevents anyone from adopting a position vulnerable to their application. The typical argument, therefore, tends to center on the applicability of proposed principles, rather than their validity.

It should be remembered, of course, that *arguing* either the applicability or inapplicability of a principle is not by a long shot the same thing as *establishing* it. Typically, the target audience (if there is one) will feel the tug of the principle, yet be open to the suggestion that it doesn't apply in these particular circumstances. Unless convincing reasons are put forward for its inapplicability, however, a familiar principle is quite likely to prevail after all. We belong to a temperamentally conservative species, and principles—those great guides to correct conclusions amid the shifting sands of circumstance —exert a powerful hold on us. We are programmed, so to speak, to regard them highly.

MARSHALING THE FACTS: EXPERT EVIDENCE

Whether we base our argument on some fundamental principle or seek to distinguish the situation in question from those to which a given principle applies, or whether this is one of those rarer cases in which we propose to attack the principle itself as invalid, it will ordinarily also be necessary to marshal and present facts in aid of our case.

Facts come in various sizes—or perhaps I should say in varying degrees of specific gravity. Some are absolutely fatal to a particular line of argument; others are the featheriest of makeweights, useful only as a sort of maraschino cherry perched atop an argument comprised of more substantial elements. And of course there are factual arguments of all intermediate degrees of impact as well.

Let us consider first one of the heavyweights of the factual class: expert evidence. This is treated in some analyses of the art of argumentation as one form of the so-called Argument from Authority, and in its higher and more rarefied forms is almost indistinguishable from the enunciation of a principle. A good example of this would be the citing of Washington's Farewell Address as authority for the proposition that the United States ought to steer clear of "entangling alliances" with the nations of the Old World.

As a matter of fact, there are times when an expert can be invoked to establish not merely a fact but a veritable principle. That is why, on the "Advocates" program concerning capital punishment, I called as my first witness Reverend Bruce A. Williams, a Dominican priest and assistant professor of moral philosophy at St. John's University. (I was arguing in favor of the states restoring capital punishment, in appropriate cases.)

Ordinarily a principle does not need to be "established"; a fact generally must. A principle will be recognized as such by the audience, and as already noted the discussion will usually turn on its applicability rather than its existence or validity. But if a principle's validity is to be attacked, or if the existence of a different governing principle in a technical field is to be contended for, an expert can often do the job best. Father Williams had, in a sense, both assignments.

It is widely assumed, whenever capital punishment is under discussion, that if theological considerations are to be invoked at all, they will weigh against it: The theologian, surely, will favor "mercy." But the situation is rather more complicated than that, as Father Williams explained on my direct examination of him. I set it forth here because I have never seen a more difficult or superficially less-appealing point involving the establishment of a principle put more persuasively:

WILLIAMS: "In my own view, the underlying principle [supporting the death penalty] would be the principle of retributive justice; and this needs to be explained, especially since nowadays it's rather largely misconceived. By retributive justice I don't mean the animalistic indulgence in personal spite or maliciousness against an offender. What I mean, rather, is that there are certain important social values—to begin with, the right to life—which must be upheld for the sake of an orderly society, and that those who affront these values by their violent behavior must be called to account for their actions by proportionate punishment. So that, for example, in the case of someone who deliberately takes a life, our willingness to impose the death penalty is our testimony to how seriously we take the value he has offended against. . . . I see nothing brutal about treating a person as a responsible agent who can be held accountable for his acts and requiring that he sustain a burden proportionate to the burden he has wrongly inflicted upon others. Quite the contrary. I think what is brutalizing and dehumanizing is to overthrow our principle of retributive justice and, in effect, treat the criminal as less than a responsible agent—as some sort of behavioral animal who is not really responsible and culpable for his crimes, who has to be treated and cured but not punished."

This was powerful stuff, but I knew that the audience would still be curious to know Father Williams' views on the role of mercy. So I anticipated the opposition's attack by raising the notion of "mercy" myself:

RUSHER: "And finally, sir, how do you square the death penalty with the Christian concept of mercy?"

WILLIAMS: "We can't even have a concept of mercy if we don't have a principle of retributive justice to begin with. There first has to be an understanding that offenses demand punishments. And once we have a principle like this, then [there can be] mercy on the part of a governor or whoever can relax the strict requirements of justice in an individual case. But if we try to codify the notion of mercy without a sense of retributive justice in the first place, we don't have mercy; we have sentimentality."

Harvard Law professor Alan Dershowitz, who was my adversary on this occasion, was unable to shake Father Williams on cross-examination:

DERSHOWITZ: "Mercy may very well require retribution, but it surely doesn't require the death penalty, does it? One could have mercy without a death penalty."

WILLIAMS: "I don't think we can have retribution adequately unless there is some notion of a proportion between the burden we are inflicting on the offender and the burden he has imposed."

DERSHOWITZ: "Well, today we think of the death penalty as the supreme penalty. There was a time, not many years ago, when we routinely imposed torture on those who tortured. Would you sustain that as retributive and proportionate?"

WILLIAMS: "I doubt if we routinely imposed it. You mean it's been done in the history of civilization."

DERSHOWITZ: "It's been done for people who have tortured."

WILLIAMS: "My view is not, Mr. Dershowitz, that every circumstance of the crime has to be imitated by every circumstance of the punishment—"

DERSHOWITZ: "Why the killing?"

WILLIAMS: "This is not always even possible. For instance, if a man has murdered three times, he cannot be executed three times."

DERSHOWITZ: "But why must we kill him?"

WILLIAMS: "Because I think the value of life is a value that of itself transcends the value of freedom, property, what-have-you."

DERSHOWITZ: "Isn't that only because we, today, regard capital punishment as the supreme penalty? If we were to regard life imprisonment as the supreme penalty, wouldn't that be enough to serve as retribution for killing?"

WILLIAMS: "I'm not too sure it's correct to say that our regard for capital punishment as a supreme penalty is a uniquely contemporary phenomenon. It was argued centuries ago, in fact, by reputable Christian philosophers, that the thing a man naturally fears to lose most is his life. And it would seem that to impose no greater penalty on a person who has deliberately taken a life than upon a person who has committed an obviously lesser offense is to, in effect, equate the value with the value of these other things."

Fortunately most authorities, however towering, are not quite so towering as God or George Washington, and the argument from authority, or submission of expert evidence, is ordinarily encountered not in the form of a bid to assert an unassailable principle but as powerful support for a factual aspect of one's case.

We have recently become familiar with this sort of factual expertise in the argument over the safety of nuclear power plants. The vast majority of people know almost nothing about the techniques for generating electric power by means of nuclear energy, and a fair proportion of them are positively frightened by the whole subject to one degree or another. The mushroom-shaped cloud over Hiroshima, with 75,000 lying dead beneath it, ushered in the nuclear era, and nuclear energy is inextricably associated in the public mind with notions of overwhelming and highly destructive force. In addition, the very nature of radiation—the fact that its emanations cannot always be perceived by our senses, yet can easily be fatal—puts us in awe of it; and matters are certainly not made any easier by the further fact that one of the longer-range consequences of overexposure to radiation may be cancer.

The ground is thus inevitably laid for a Battle of the Experts: experts who affirm that nuclear energy is not only the cheapest but the cleanest and the safest means of generating electric power, and other experts who declare that it will inevitably result, under ordinary operation, in unacceptably high levels of background radiation, and—far worse—that there is a real danger of accidents which may rupture the containing walls surrounding the reactor core and, by wind and other means, spread nuclear wastes across an area "the size of the state of Pennsylvania," killing thousands of people outright.

Strictly as a matter of rhetoric, practically all of the high cards

82

here are in the hands of the critics of nuclear energy. They have
going for them not only the public's ignorance and deep fear of nuclear energy—which many honorable advocates will not wish to fan,
but which can hardly harm their cause—but also that profoundly
conservative instinct in mankind that tends to oppose any proposed
course of action that *might* result in harm.

No responsible supporter of nuclear energy can be found who will
argue that a catastrophic accident simply *could not possibly* happen
at a nuclear power plant. A combination of natural calamities and
human errors is theoretically conceivable which would indeed have
the devastating effect described by nuclear power's foes. All that its
supporters can do is point to the precautions taken (e.g., the concrete containment walls three or four feet thick, reinforced with steel
bars as thick as beer cans), the impressive safety record of commercial nuclear power (not a single radiation-related fatality in the entire thirty-year history of the American industry), and the cost in
human lives of a "worst-case" scenario, averaged over the time span
within which one such "worst case" may reasonably be expected to
occur, compared with the cost in human lives of other forms of
power generation. (One Ford Foundation study, for example, esti-
mates that if a catastrophic accident occurred at a nuclear power
plant somewhere in America once in a century, it might kill as many
as 10,000 victims immediately, plus 15,000 more over longer periods.
It goes on to note, however, that these are fewer innocent victims
than will predictably die in railroad-crossing accidents involving coal-
carrying freight trains during the same century.)

Say what they will, however, the proponents of nuclear power
have, rhetorically speaking, the short end of the stick. It is no doubt
true that an average of 140 miners die every year in this country in
coal-mine accidents; or, to put it another way, that it costs the lives
of two uranium miners to produce a billion megawatts of electricity
by means of nuclear energy, versus the lives of 179 coal miners to
produce the same amount of electricity in coal-fired plants. But mine
accidents are a comparatively familiar phenomenon, and the deaths
are widely distributed in both space and time. It may even be true,
as other recent studies report, that ordinary background radiation—
from cosmic rays, rock formations, French and Chinese nuclear tests,

chest and dental X rays, etc.—will cause the death by cancer of some 220,000 members of the current U.S. population, and that radiation from nuclear power plants can be expected to increase that figure by only about 2,000, or less than 1 percent. But the other sources of low-level radiation are either unavoidable or practically so, whereas nuclear power is often depicted as simply one option among many.

In short, proponents of nuclear power can argue until they are blue in the face without quite eliminating that "But what if" from the human mind. In the circumstances, as an advocate of nuclear power, I have found it necessary to proceed slowly and deliberately, bringing the hidden fears of the audience to the surface and trying to confront them rationally: pointing out that we are not being offered a simple choice between safety and danger, but a choice between energy systems all of which cost lives. (The same, of course, is true of alternative transportation systems, and here again we encounter the curious human preference for widely spaced deaths, no matter how numerous: It is a truism that flying in commercial airliners is much safer than traveling in private cars, yet we coolly countenance the loss of tens of thousands of innocent lives every year on America's roads—not to mention risking our own—while a surprisingly large number of people can scarcely bring themselves to fly.)

For our present purposes, the lessons to be drawn from this short tour of the argument over nuclear power are several. First, expert evidence is useful in direct proportion to the self-recognized ignorance of the target audience or opponent. (I say "self-recognized" ignorance because, of course, if the ignorance is unrecognized, the tendency to listen to an authority on the subject is diminished.) Expert evidence is thus highly useful in arguments over such public issues as nuclear power, SALT negotiations and disarmament generally, economic policies (especially of the broader sort—farmers, for example, don't need experts to tell them about parity), problems involving the internal affairs of foreign nations, etc. Expertise is, conversely, less useful where the average man, or at any rate the opponent or target audience, considers that his own background information is reasonably adequate. That is why many hot arguments over civil rights, the various "lib" movements, the Vietnam war (save perhaps in its more

84

technical military aspects), forced busing, etc., seldom involve expert
evidence and in any event rarely turn on it.

In business arguments, or in comparable situations below the level
of national issues, the expert can be just as effective as in a debate
over SALT II. In my own business, which is the publishing of *National Review* magazine, the recognized expertise of my associate
publisher, Jim McFadden, in all matters pertaining to circulation
promotion can often end an argument almost before it has begun.
The final decision may technically rest with Bill Buckley as owner, or
in his absence with me; but McFadden's word is very nearly law in
his special field. Shall a particular promotion drive be undertaken?
Shall newsstand sales be expanded, or dropped altogether? Shall the
price of a year's subscription be raised another dollar? Shall current
subscribers first be offered an opportunity to renew at the old price?
Other things being equal, McFadden's opinion on all these questions
will be decisive, since he is the acknowledged resident expert. Normally, the only possibility of challenging him would be with the
opinion of some other alleged expert—the reported experience, for
example, of some other publication.

And that brings us to the second lesson: The best and often the
only counter to expert evidence is rival expert evidence. This is frequently on display in legal proceedings, where opposing psychiatrists
in a homicide case will solemnly swear that the killer was (or wasn't)
legally sane, and opposing surgeons in a malpractice suit will testify
that a particular medical procedure was (or wasn't) an acceptable
and prudent treatment. On "The Advocates," my opponents and I
so regularly deployed contradictory expert testimony that, in a burst
of exasperated cynicism, I once formulated as a solemn rule the proposition that "a scientist, economist, or clergyman can always be
found who will take any position desired in the fields of their respective expertise." That may be overstating the case, but not much.

In any event, if his adversary is using expert evidence in an appropriate situation, the competent arguer will often feel compelled to do
likewise, as a necessary form of counterbattery.

A third lesson is that expert evidence can be, and sometimes must
be, used to counter natural fears of the unknown—nuclear energy
being a spectacular example, but by no means the only one.

A fourth lesson involves the necessary limitations of expert evidence. However imposing it is, it will rarely induce anybody to subordinate his own critical capacities altogether, no matter how profound his own ignorance. People respect experts, but seldom blindly. Experts too are human, and have been known to err—witness the towering authority on handwriting who quite mistakenly identified as the authentic signature of Howard Hughes what later turned out to be one of Clifford Irving's forgeries.

It is probably needless to say that cross-examining an expert, or in the broader sense even arguing with one, involves risks and problems all its own. In a courtroom the time-honored rule, though perhaps more honored in the breach than the observance, is, "Never ask a question to which you do not know and cannot compel the answer." That is, however, a counsel of perfection. There will be times when an expert must be challenged, not by the presentation of an opposing expert, but directly by the opposing adversary himself and under circumstances when it may not always be possible to compel a particular answer.

In such a situation, the best of all possible worlds is to be able to confront the expert with his own previous statements—statements at odds with those he is making and defending in the present argument. This opportunity is not necessarily as rare as you might suppose: Experts perforce go on record more than the rest of us, and a search of the records may yield surprising results. (Hence, no doubt, the familiar epigram, "O, that my adversary may have written a book!")

Once on "The Advocates," when I was preparing to defend the desirability of import quotas on textiles and shoes, my team of researchers and I were advised that the principal witness for the opposition would be Paul Samuelson, the MIT economist, who only a few months before had been awarded the Nobel prize for economics. My heart sank; for in addition to the obvious difficulties of trying to cross-examine such an overwhelming authority, economics is a subject I had long detested precisely because it is so amorphous that "experts" in it can take any position they wish with relatively little danger of being caught in some apparent contradiction not capable of being explained away.

One of my researchers, however, had discovered in Professor Samuelson's famous textbook, *Economics*, a statement that seemed to suggest that workers thrown out of work in an unprotected industry might well become chronically unemployed. This contradicted the position he was taking on the program (i.e., that they are usually promptly employed in some other, more efficient industry), and in my cross-examination of him I intended to make the most of that fact. Samuelson, however, was a sly old fox, as the transcript of my interrogation makes clear:

RUSHER: "In your book, *Economics*, page 656 in the eighth edition, you spoke of the 'theory of comparative advantage,' which I gather underlies the free-trade principle you're arguing for here, and said that 'it *pretends* [my emphasis] that when workers go out of one industry, they always go into another more efficient industry, and never into chronic unemployment.' I take it that the thrust of that was that very frequently they do in fact go into chronic unemployment?"

SAMUELSON: "No, I think that what is said there is that its major premise is that macroeconomic fiscal and monetary policies assure high employment opportunities, and then they will go from one industry into the other."

RUSHER: "Then what is it that 'pretends' that they do, when in fact they don't? You used the word 'pretend'—'that if workers go out of one industry, they always go into another.'"

SAMUELSON: "Yes, but let me stand corrected then. It 'assumes' . . ."

Muted though my victory was by Samuelson's sensible concession, made in a distinctly minor key, I felt more than a little proud to have compelled a Nobel prize-winner in economics to admit there was a technical misstatement in the eighth edition of his famous textbook on the subject!

If the expert under attack cannot be found to have made some usefully contradictory statement on a previous occasion, he can at least often be tempted into minor but nonetheless debilitating concessions. If he has been presented as an authority for point A, he may nevertheless be induced to concede that there are circumstances under which point A is not true, or that the support for it, while substantial, is not overwhelming, etc. This was the problem faced by

the attorney for the defense in the Jascalevich murder case in New
Jersey in 1978 (best remembered, perhaps, as the case in which a
New York *Times* reporter, M. A. Farber, was jailed for contempt of
court for refusing to turn over his interview notes on various
witnesses for the judge's review). The defendant was a physician accused of having murdered several patients ten or twelve years earlier,
by inserting a potent drug called curare into their veins. The bodies had been exhumed, and expert witnesses for the prosecution had
testified that traces of curare had been found in several of them.

Since Dr. Jascalevich had admitted possessing curare at the time,
purportedly in connection with certain tests he was conducting on
animals, this was clearly very deadly testimony, and his lawyer spent
long hours cross-examining the experts on the point. Normally, they
admitted, curare is difficult to identify in a body after so long a time;
but a certain new chemical test makes it possible to do so, and had
yielded positive results in the case of several of the exhumed bodies.
Jascalevich's counsel worked heroically to wring concessions from the
hostile experts: that the new tests were not invariably accurate; that
the results obtained were not altogether decisive; etc. And he may
well have succeeded to some degree, for the jury acquitted Dr. Jascalevich.

In questioning an expert, another thing to bear in mind is that
his own consciousness of his reputation as an expert may sometimes
be used against him. A real expert, after all, is normally aware and
proud of his expertise, and on guard to defend it against successful
impeachment. He will not, therefore, usually be in a mood to just
"say anything" that will win a point. If, on cross-examination, he is
treated with due respect, he may be tempted into admitting to
doubts or views that his sponsors fervently wish he did not have.

That was the trap that Howard Miller, my opponent on "The Advocates," laid for my witness, Leo Cherne, on a program debating
whether the government should drop the charges against Daniel Ellsberg for leaking the so-called Pentagon Papers to the press. Cherne,
executive director of the Research Institute of America, and also
chairman of the executive committee of Freedom House, was
offered, if not precisely as an expert on the subject, at least as a pres-
tigious moderate liberal whose views were entitled to special respect

precisely because he was known to be a fair-minded supporter of the general principles of free speech. Cherne was rightly determined to appear and to be balanced and judicious under cross-examination, and Miller exploited this determination brilliantly by inviting him to cling to his position (that people who publish classified documents must be punished) in a different and far more difficult situation:

MILLER: "Mr. Cherne, let's talk about uniform enforcement. Should ex-President Johnson be prosecuted because he released some of the same classified material [i.e., material appearing in the Pentagon Papers] in his book [published by] Holt, Rinehart and Winston?"

CHERNE: "I deplore the actions of Presidents and assistants to Presidents. I deplore—"

MILLER: "But is it your position that ex-President Johnson should in fact be prosecuted?"

CHERNE: "No, it is not; no, it is clearly not."

MILLER: "Well, why not? He released classified documents."

CHERNE: "Let me say why not. First of all it would be virtually impossible for a President, having sat at the very center of every fundamental decision of the years in which he was in office, to even live and breathe—"

MILLER: "The same documents—"

CHERNE: "Live and breathe—"

MILLER: "Documents, Mr. Cherne. Let's be clear what we're talking about. Mr. Bradley's affidavit says the same documents are in the Johnson book. Should President Johnson be prosecuted?"

Cherne actually stammered as he began his reply, so painful was the concession Miller was wringing from him. But Cherne had taken his stand as a matter of principle, and the best he could think to do on the spur of the moment was to adhere to it doggedly in all circumstances:

CHERNE: "By the application of my principle, I would have to say yes."

MILLER: "Thank you."

The trouble, of course, was that this particular application of the principle was patently absurd, yet Miller, by successfully tempting Cherne to defend it, had managed to suggest to the audience that other applications of the same principle might either be equally absurd or, at the very best, capriciously and unfairly selective.

Of course Cherne undoubtedly conceived himself as being impaled on the horns of a dilemma: Either he had to apply the principle to Johnson, or stand convicted of unjust discrimination. But no doubt he realized later (these realizations have a most unsatisfactory way of coming too late) that he could easily have denied Miller any meaningful victory by some such reply as, "Come on now, Mr. Miller. A handful of presidential memos, which are what Johnson printed, are hardly to be compared to forty-seven volumes of government documents. Besides, it was President Johnson under whose authority those memos had been classified in the first place. What he could classify, he presumably could—and in effect did—declassify."

But Miller had rightly sensed Cherne's high-minded determination to apply the relevant principle altogether uniformly, without reference to narrower considerations, and managed to score effectively because of it.

Even more effective, of course, are those occasions on which an expert can be persuaded to admit that he actually doesn't agree, at least fully, with the case he is being offered as supporting. That was the situation on an "Advocates" program debating whether public employees at the state and local level ought to have the right to strike. The extreme cases which are most difficult for proponents of this right are those involving policemen and firemen, whose work involves protection of the public in life-threatening emergency situations. One of Miller's witnesses was to be the New York labor attorney and frequent impartial arbitrator, Theodore Kheel. My team got wind of a rumor that Kheel, while ready to defend strikes by public employees in most cases, had doubts about it in the case of policemen and firemen. I moved quickly to the sore spot in opening my cross-examination:

RUSHER: "Mr. Kheel, it is of some importance, given the relation that you have to the labor situation in New York, for us to know: Do you favor, after a 'cooling-off period,' as you call it—analogous to the eighty-day injunction available in private cases of emergency under the Taft-Hartley Law—a right of the police to strike?"

KHEEL: "I think the right to strike has to be viewed in its context.

It has no significance today in collective bargaining apart from the right to bargain collectively. Now I would, nevertheless, provide at the end of the collective bargaining line a mechanism for the protection of the public. Undoubtedly, in most, if not all, instances that mechanism would be invoked to prevent a strike by policemen."

RUSHER: "Mr. Kheel, forgive me for forcing the issue, but then you do disagree with the proposal as framed by Mr. Miller?"

KHEEL: "No, I don't. What we are looking at is the right to bargain collectively. And I would impose any restrictions on the right to bargain collectively at the end of the bargaining line. The Taylor Law prohibits strikes in all cases, under all circumstances, and for all time, and therefore frustrates collective bargaining in all cases."

Kheel, in short, favored letting public employees strike in most (but not all) cases. I wanted, however, to discuss the others.

RUSHER: "You see, sir, it is the difficult cases that we're focusing on here at the moment. The police and the firemen are the two most difficult cases."

KHEEL: "Why should all of collective bargaining be frustrated because of the difficult cases?"

RUSHER: "I'm not saying it should. I think, however, that Mr. Miller—"

KHEEL: "Yes, you are."

RUSHER: "Now just a moment. If Mr. Miller is going to propose, as he has proposed, and has reiterated a moment ago he does propose, an unlimited right to strike by police and firemen after the eighty-day period, and you don't favor that, I'm entitled to introduce you to Mr. Miller and observe that you have a little discussing to do between yourselves."

KHEEL: "I think that as we get along that you will find that there is no conflict between us."

RUSHER: "Well, I certainly find some now."

KHEEL: "We are talking about the right to bargain collectively. We are not talking about the exceptional circumstances. And what you do is to take an exceptional circumstance, project it, and thereby frustrate the right to bargain collectively for 95 percent of public employees."

RUSHER: "Mr. Kheel, it's an artistic job, but the fact of the matter is that you are not here, apparently, tonight prepared to argue for the right of the police or the firemen to strike, and I don't blame you. Neither am I; but Mr. Miller is."

KHEEL: "I am arguing—"

Moderator Victor Palmieri was now moved to intervene:

PALMIERI: "Well, gentlemen, let's try to clarify—"

RUSHER: "Yes."

PALMIERI: "Mr. Kheel, I think that the point that Mr. Rusher is pressing you on, for the purpose of this program, is a fair point. I think we need to know what qualifications you're asserting for the unlimited right to strike with respect to these two critical public professions. Please comply."

KHEEL: "Well, I would not confine it to these two critical ones. There may be others. For example, if a public employer runs an electric utility, it may well be that a strike in such circumstances might be so severe as to be subject to prohibition. But I would put the process of prohibition at the very end of the line. I would not start out by saying that police and firemen don't have the right to strike."

PALMIERI: "Well, I must say that I'm confused now. Why would that be true with respect to that class of employees but perhaps not to, say, nurses in a private hospital whose strike might cause the death of patients?"

KHEEL: "It might well be. You have to take these cases up on an *ad hoc* basis. You have two rights—"

RUSHER: "May I ask a question?"

PALMIERI: "I'll let you ask a question, Mr. Rusher."

KHEEL: "—two rights that may be in conflict with each other. One is the right to bargain collectively, and the other is the right of the public to be protected in its health and safety. The thing to do is to try to balance these rights so that you get the maximum protection in both cases. If you start out with a total prohibition on strikes by public employees, then you have eliminated collective bargaining in all cases."

RUSHER: "Mr. Kheel, I'll stipulate that you agree with Mr. Miller in part and with me in part and go to another question instead."

Having established some distance between Miller's position and

Kheel's, I took care to stress it as the debate went on. An opportunity arose a few minutes later:

KHEEL: "You can't measure strikes simply by their numbers. It's a matter of their impact. But unfortunately, and I say this with great regret, we have had more serious strikes in New York since the Taylor Law was passed than ever before."

RUSHER: "Including a police strike just recently."

KHEEL: "Yes, including a police strike."

RUSHER: "One of those that you would close down but Mr. Miller would not."

And I underlined the point again in my summation:

RUSHER: "It occurs to me that we might arrange for a little collective bargaining between Mr. Kheel, who favors preventing police strikes, enjoining them, and Mr. Miller and his film man, who has shown us this passionate film on why policemen should be allowed to strike. In any case, tonight the opposition, or at least that part of it represented by Mr. Miller, confronts us with the proposition that the right to strike should be expanded to include the right of the police to walk off their jobs and let the criminals take over."

In discussing the use of experts and quasi experts to establish a fact (or even a principle), and some of the techniques available to counter them, I have cited chiefly examples drawn from "Advocates" debates; but the same general rules apply in all arguments, however informal. An expert is an expert, whether he is a Nobel prize-winning economist, or an office colleague with recognized expertise in a given field, or an uncle whom everybody in the family acknowledges as authoritative, either in general or in some particular. In all three cases, the techniques for countering him remain the same: Invoke higher or equal authority to the contrary; obtain concessions as to the significance of the adduced fact; rely on his pride in his own expertise to maneuver him toward a middle ground; etc.

MARSHALING THE FACTS: ATTACKING AN OPPONENT'S FACTS

So much for experts. With regard to an opponent's presentation of facts in general, whether adduced with the help of an expert or in any other way (e.g., by citing a newspaper article or a neighbor's report), the two fundamental lines of attack parallel those used in attacking a principle: If possible, either challenge its truth or deny its relevance.

Challenging an asserted fact's truth may be downright impossible, but if at all possible, it is worth doing in direct proportion to the importance the fact has in an opponent's argumentation. For example, in a 1973 book entitled *Amnesty? Now! Never! If . . .* (Sun River Press), I participated in a three-way written debate on the issue of amnesty for Vietnam draft-evaders and deserters with Arlie Schardt of the American Civil Liberties Union and Senator Mark Hatfield of Oregon. Schardt favored immediate and unconditional amnesty; Hatfield argued for conditional amnesty; and I opposed amnesty altogether. In the course of my argumentation I laid heavy and repeated emphasis on the fact that "There has never been, in the history of the United States, a general unconditional amnesty for individuals who dodged the draft or deserted in time of war."

As it happened, neither of my adversaries was able to cite any instance of an amnesty that contradicted that factual assertion; but it is easy to see how damaging to my case such an example would have been. I was hinging my argument heavily (though, of course, not exclusively) on a historical analysis that, as I presented it, was almost tantamount to a governing principle. A successful attack on the asserted fact would have been correspondingly effective.*

Similarly, one extremely telling argument in favor of nuclear power is stated factually as follows: "There has never been, in the entire history of this country, a single radiation-related fatality in a commercial nuclear-power plant." One must take care to put the point exactly that way, or it ceases to be true: There have been a modest number of such fatalities in *other* countries; there have been a few *non-radiation-related* fatalities in commercial nuclear-power plants in this country (e.g., two men were killed by the explosion of an ordinary steam pipe); and there have been a number of radiation-related deaths (about seven, I believe) at *non-commercial* plants in

---

* President Carter's 1976 campaign pledge of amnesty for Vietnam evaders and deserters seemed likely to eliminate the historical argument thenceforth, but as matters turned out it did so only partially. Mr. Carter ultimately pardoned only draft evaders—not deserters.

this country (i.e., military installations, most of them in the early days of the industry when safeguards were fewer). Finally, it is always possible to argue that there *will* be a link between some accident such as Three Mile Island, in which small amounts of radioactive steam were vented, and cases of cancer in the vicinity ten or twenty years hence. (HEW Secretary Califano's revised estimate is that one such death will occur at some future time as a result of Three Mile Island.)

Still, the factual statement remains true as of the moment this is written, and it is a powerful argument in favor of nuclear energy, especially when one considers the high and inexorable toll in human lives taken by coal and other alternative forms of energy. By the same token, however, the first exception to the rule—the first life actually claimed by radiation at an American commercial nuclear-power plant—will, if and when it occurs (and I suppose we might as well say "when" because surely one will occur sooner or later), have a correspondingly powerful impact on public opinion. The opponents of nuclear power are now forced to confine themselves to supportive hypotheses; when they are offered supportive facts instead, they will assuredly use them.

In arguments of the more formal type—legal proceedings, college or television debates, etc.—a fact will rarely be asserted if it is open to challenge as to its truth: There is too much temptation for the adversary to explore and undermine it with devastating consequences. In informal arguments around the office or home, however, "facts" are often asserted with less precision. A beautiful illustration, involving a colloquy that scarcely rose to the dignity of an argument, is cherished in my recollection as the anecdote of "Bill Buckley and the Honda."

At one point in middle age, when he might legitimately be assumed to have known better, Buckley took to riding a motorcycle between his office and his Manhattan apartment. His contention was that it was the perfect solution to New York's ghastly traffic problems; and no doubt in its way it was. At all events, Buckley was soon a familiar if slightly startling sight to passersby on Park Avenue, maneuvering his beloved Honda in and out of traffic.

There was, however, the little problem of parking the blasted thing. At home this was relatively easy to solve, since Bill's ground-floor apartment had its own entrance from the street and the gleaming black monster could be put in the vestibule. The office, however, was another matter. Parking the motorcycle on the street or just inside the building's glass doors, where it could be seen by anyone passing, was obviously too great a temptation to thieves and vandals. So Bill took to leaving it in the small corridor on an upper floor, off which are doors leading to various suites of offices, including his.

This was, of course, technically a fire hazard, since the corridor was legally required to be left unobstructed in case of an emergency —in fact, a lawyer with a suite on the same floor was heard to say as much.

Nonetheless, the Honda remained there, day after day, while Bill's infatuation with this new toy wore itself away. One day as I was leaving the building for lunch I glanced at it for the umpteenth time and my mind was still on the subject when I encountered Bill on the ground floor, just arriving from somewhere. Trying to look suitably lawyerly, I broached the subject afresh:

"Really, Bill, you ought to park your Honda somewhere else. Leaving it in the corridor is flatly against Fire Department regulations."

To which Bill smilingly replied over his shoulder, as he disappeared into the elevator:

"I talked to the Fire Commissioner, and he says it's all right."

I had been deflated before in my life, but never quite that thoroughly. I had piled my entire case on a fire regulation; but Buckley, who knows everybody from Henry Kissinger to Margaret Thatcher on a first-name basis, had turned my flank by a little private tête-à-tête with the Fire Commissioner!

Over lunch I brooded on the matter. Was it possible—really possible—that New York's Fire Commissioner could be gulled, at some cocktail party, into suspending, at least in this instance, a departmental regulation designed, after all, to save lives? I resolved to look into the matter more closely; and I quickly discovered that Buckley's factual assertion was, to put it charitably, full of holes: (1) It wasn't Buckley himself who had talked to the Fire Commissioner, but Buckley's personal chauffeur (Bill maintained a car too, for occasions when the Honda wouldn't do); (2) the chauffeur hadn't talked directly to the Fire Commissioner, but to some aide in the Commissioner's office; and (3) the aide *hadn't* said it was "all right" to park the Honda in the corridor!

Moral: Inspect dubious factual assertions, especially in informal contexts.

Finally, one must be on guard against the factual assertion that once was, or appeared to be, true, but which is now much less clearly true. Consider the recent history of the claims for and against marijuana. For thirty years, until the early 1960s, it was extravagantly denounced by Federal Narcotics chief Harry Anslinger as a "killer weed," which millions of experimenters soon discovered for themselves it was not. Marijuana thus actually benefited from Anslinger's exaggerated descriptions of its consequences. In the early 1970s the report of the President's Commission on Marijuana swung to the other extreme, asserting in effect that marijuana in moderation was, medically speaking, harmless. Relying on this imposing assurance, marijuana advocates made spectacular headway in promoting its use and, in certain jurisdictions, even decriminalizing it.

By the mid-1970s, however, new medical evidence, adduced by the World Health Organization, various British researchers, and America's own National Institute on Drug Abuse, had pushed the wildly gyrating pendulum back toward—or beyond—center. It now seems established that the principal hallucinogenic agent in marijuana—tetrahydrocannabinol, or THC—is absorbed by the body's fatty tissues (including the brain and gonads) and lingers there far longer than alcohol remains in the system. Precisely what damage this does, if any, and how much are still hotly contested issues; but anybody who hereafter wants to conduct, on either side, a serious argument about the medical effects of marijuana should take care to equip himself with the latest data.

In general, the demonstration that one of an adversary's factual assertions is untrue has a double impact: Not only is that particular factual support for his argument removed, but in a more general way the credibility of the entire remainder of his factual presentation is undermined. If he has erred in one demonstrated instance, either innocently or otherwise, how can anyone be sure he has not erred in others as well? That is why a competent arguer will take great care to make sure that his factual assertions are unchallengeable—more care, even, than might seem to be warranted by their actual significance as part of his case.

If, however, a factual assertion is unassailably correct, it may still be as vulnerable as a sound principle to the charge of inapplicability or (as we say in the case of facts) irrelevance. The fact that a murder suspect's alibi for Saturday is unshakable may be quite true—but irrelevant if the murder was committed on Sunday.

Such cut-and-dried instances of factual irrelevance have a convenient way of being so obvious that they usually take care of themselves. But we enter more slippery terrain when we encounter the fact that is *partially* relevant. If, as George Tyrrell charged, the Jesuits, when accused of killing three men and a dog, "triumphantly produce the dog alive," their factual rebuttal plainly is relevant to only a portion of the charge. (On the other hand, in fairness to the Jesuits, whoever made the charge was plainly wrong with regard to a portion of it; hasn't his over-all credibility been damaged to some extent? It may have been easier for the Jesuits to lay hands on and produce the animal they were accused of killing than to find and produce three alleged human victims, who may not want to be found and produced.)

As a really spectacular example of a factual assertion that was offered as the basic underpinning of a contention, but was actually (and in this serpentine case was even intended to be) largely, though invisibly, irrelevant, I offer the following from my extensive file on Richard M. Nixon. If liberal readers have had to endure an oversupply of illustrations selected at the expense of some of their favorite people and policies, I hope this one will go far in the direction of compensating the imbalance.

Late in 1957, shortly after I came to *National Review*, Bill Buckley received through Ralph de Toledano an invitation to interview Richard Nixon, then Eisenhower's Vice-President. Nixon was, of course, already the acknowledged front-runner for the 1960 Republican presidential nomination. Buckley, as founder and editor of *National Review*, was one of the best known spokesmen of the new conservative wave in American political thought. The encounter, therefore, while in formal terms an "interview," was far more than a typical meeting between a politician and a journalist; it had the elements of an encounter between a candidate and a political bloc that might or might not decide to support him.

Buckley asked me to suggest "some hard questions" for Nixon, and I mulled the problem over carefully. Ordinarily I consider it futile to ask questions of an adept politician, but here there would be, as there so rarely is even in a presidential press conference, an opportunity to pursue any important point to any desired length. The interview was to take place in Nixon's home (later changed to his office, but with the same ambience of lack of pressure carefully retained); only Nixon, Buckley and de Toledano (a friend of both men) would be present; and there would be no time limit whatever.

I considered and dismissed any question that would merely seek to impale Nixon on a dilemma whose two horns consisted of conventional liberal and conservative positions: Nixon presented himself, in the politics of the Eisenhower era, as a moderate conservative. Seven times out of ten he could and would seek to satisfy Buckley with a moderately conservative response; on the other three occasions he could afford to adopt downright liberal positions, confident that his over-all score, so to speak, would remain fairly high.

I should add here that, at that particular moment, one wing of liberal opinion was still of the opinion that Richard Nixon might yet be useful to their cause. James Reston in particular (who had argued, prophetically and rightly, to his fellow liberals at the outset of the Eisenhower administration that "the battle for the mind of President Eisenhower is not yet lost") was publicly of this opinion. Marquis Childs, on the other hand, was a leading spokesman for the contrary view: i.e., that Nixon was, from the liberal standpoint at least, irredeemable.

What was needed then, was not a question that would merely force Nixon to choose between the liberals and *us*, but one that would force him to choose between the liberals and *Eisenhower*: some issue, in other words, on which Eisenhower and the liberals sharply disagreed, and about which the liberals cared deeply. Nixon, as Eisenhower's Vice-President and would-be successor, simply did not dare to disagree publicly with his chief on anything—least of all to adopt a position more liberal than Ike's. Their relationship, always delicate, must not be put to such a dreadful test. On the other hand, to endorse publicly a conservative position of Eisenhower's about which liberals felt strongly would offer maximum offense to the liberals. But was there such a position?

Luckily there was. Eisenhower had appointed a special blue-ribbon board, headed by former Army Secretary Gordon Gray, to advise him on whether or not to revoke the security clearance of J. Robert Oppenheimer, the noted nuclear physicist. Oppenheimer, who had been deeply involved in constructing the first atomic bomb during World War II, had subsequently, during the height of the Cold War with the Soviet Union, opposed the construction of the hydrogen bomb, and the charge had been made that this opposition reflected his political sympathies. The Gray Board, sifting the evidence, which included contributions to the Communist Party by Oppenheimer early in the 1940s, had concluded that his clearance ought indeed to be revoked. Eisenhower, though he had not yet acted, was known to agree. (He did, in fact, subsequently revoke Oppenheimer's clearance.)

Meanwhile, the whole subject had become a major issue for many liberals. The covers of both *Harper's* and *The Atlantic* featured articles on the subject. Columnists and editorial writers weighed in with their views. It was quite a brouhaha. And it provided, I thought, the perfect question for Buckley to ask Nixon: Did the Vice-President think Dr. Oppenheimer's security clearance ought to be revoked, as recommended by the Gray Board?

There was, so far as I could see, no easy exit for Nixon from the dilemma this question posed. Either he did think so—in which case liberals, including such near-recruits as Reston, would be aghast; or he didn't—in which case Eisenhower would be furious (and Ike's rages, I am told, were of the cumulonimbus variety). Up to that point, it is almost needless to add, Nixon had kept silent on the question.

Buckley quickly grasped my strategy, and at a convenient moment during the session put the question. Nixon's reply was instantaneous:

"I have the highest confidence in the integrity of the Gray Board."

Instantaneous, and a masterpiece. Twenty-three years later, I still marvel at the deceptive polish of that reply. It was a simple, seem-

ingly straightforward declarative sentence. There was nothing negative, halting, or qualified about it. Moreover, it praised the Gray
Board—and thus by implication the Board's recommendation, and
thereby seemed to come down on the conservative side of the underlying question.

Here, then, is an instance of a statement of fact apparently offered
in support of a position: "The Gray Board has recommended the
revocation of Oppenheimer's clearance. I have the highest confidence in the integrity of the Gray Board." The conclusion almost screams at us: "Therefore I favor revocation." Even in this
baldly syllogistic form Nixon's assertion still seems forthright and
clear—unless we open our minds to the possibility that the Gray
Board might have been honest and yet wrong. That was a perfectly
reasonable possibility, and Mr. Nixon's statement of fact therefore
covered the necessary territory only partially, since, of course, the
fundamental question was not whether the Gray Board was *honest*
but whether its recommendation was *right*.

We may be quite sure, I think, that Nixon's answer to Buckley
was far from spontaneous. It had been carefully devised, as they say
annual corporate reports and bikinis are, to "reveal much that is interesting while concealing everything that is vital." If, however, it
was spontaneous, then so much the greater was its cleverness. In
ninety-nine cases out of a hundred, it would have sufficed. The conservative questioner would have thought he was getting a conservative answer, while Scotty Reston could later be assured privately to
the contrary. The Gray Board's integrity was indisputable, and
yet . . .

Unfortunately for Nixon, this was the hundredth case. Bill Buckley saw the loophole, and moved firmly to close it: Leaving aside
the Gray Board's integrity, or taking it for granted, did Mr. Nixon in
fact favor revoking Oppenheimer's clearance?

I am told that the ensuing cross-country chase, with the fox never
more than a few yards ahead of the hounds, lasted quite a while.
When it ended, Nixon rather sullenly committed himself to the
proposition that "revising security standards" in a way that would let
Oppenheimer's security clearance stand "would be to 'collapse' our
internal-security program."

Even this was a strange formulation, to say the least: By equating a participle and an infinitive, the latter of which described an action that was by implication undesirable, Mr. Nixon was permitting the inference that he considered the former also undesirable, and therefore would, again by implication, favor its opposite. Hardly very forthright! But Buckley rightly regarded it as news, and printed a summary of their long discussion of the subject in the very next issue of *National Review*:

> We are glad to report that Vice-President Nixon believes a) that the Gray Board which found Dr. Oppenheimer a security risk reached a conscientious decision conforming with the directives of relevant security orders; b) that nothing, in his opinion, has happened since 1954 to render obsolete the security standards with reference to which Dr. Oppenheimer's clearance was removed; and c) that revising security standards to the point where they would let through men with such a record as Dr. Oppenheimer's would be to "collapse" our internal security program. The above, ladies and gentlemen, we have from the Vice-President's own mouth.

Nixon had, in fact, done what he had to do: Offered no choice but to offend either Eisenhower or the liberals, he opted to offend the liberals. Marquis Childs promptly hailed the response in his column as proof that Nixon was not to be trusted. Reston was given Lord only knows what lame explanation by the Vice-President. All I know is that, some time later, an aide in Nixon's office whom I happened to know told me that "Buckley didn't do himself any good with the boss by printing that paragraph." When I notified Bill of this, he promptly checked with de Toledano to see if he had inadvertently broken some rule in reporting Nixon's answer. Not at all, de Toledano replied: The whole interview was "on the record," and the quoted statement was a part of it.

Moral: Look carefully at factual statements, even when they are true, to make sure that they are relevant—and relevant to the whole issue, not to just a part of it, or to some collateral question. (Look especially carefully if it is Mr. Nixon who is speaking.)

MARSHALING THE FACTS:
THE USE OF ANALOGIES

One of the commonest introductions of a factual proposition into an argument is by way of analogy. This is, in fact, one of the recognized devices of argumentation: the Argument by Analogy, and it has both its uses and its defects.

The basic effect of a valid analogy is to suggest that a given set of circumstances will have a certain result because a previous set of similar circumstances had that same result. "Don't feed the dog waffles; the last time you did that he got sick" is a modest but excellent example—drawn, I am sorry to say, not from imagination but from life. When I was a teenager our Scotty was so much one of the family that he talked us into letting him share our waffles one Sunday morning—and wound up at the vet's.

As in the example just cited, an analogy is a powerful argument indeed if the circumstances are truly similar. It becomes, however, progressively less powerful as the circumstances of the situation under discussion vary increasingly from those of the situation cited by way of analogy. And that is why the attack upon an analogy offered by an adversary in support of his case ordinarily consists of distinguishing the facts of the allegedly analogous case from the facts of this one. "Wear your rubbers; the last time you went out in the rain without them you caught pneumonia" may thus be open to the riposte, "That time I was out in the rain for an hour; this time I'm going next door." (The cited case might also, however, give rise to another line of attack on an analogy—denial of the implied cause-and-effect relationship: "That wasn't why I got pneumonia; the doctor said I had been run down for a year." There is also a third—denial of the truth of the alleged consequence: "That wasn't pneumonia; it was only a chest cold." We will deal with these types of counter-arguments shortly.)

Luckily for those who find themselves confronted with an argument by way of analogy, two sets of circumstances are seldom exactly alike. The differences can be dwelt upon and emphasized, to the detriment of the analogy. "The last time we opened a retail outlet in

Oshkosh it went broke in three months"—"Yes, but that was at the bottom of the 1973–74 recession. Besides, we opened that one in an area of the city that was on the decline. This one will be in a shopping center in the heaviest-spending residential area."

Most analogies emerge from this sort of give and take with diminished force, but their cogency is seldom destroyed altogether. Even fairly dissimilar situations can be cited with measurable effect, if they are at least faintly analogous to the case under consideration. What's more, such citations can be cumulated. I.e., if one analogy is too weak to be persuasive all by itself, two such may be more effective, and four or five may carry the day. For example, if one general wants to persuade another to carry out a flank attack rather than a frontal assault, citing MacArthur's brilliant landing behind the North Korean lines at Inchon may not do the job all by itself (if only because the general knows very well he's no MacArthur); but citing a well-chosen series of examples of successful flank attacks and disastrous frontal assaults might do the trick.

Distinguishing one situation from another, incidentally, often affords an opportunity for some of those rhetorical flourishes that constitute a part of the art of advocacy. To return to our homespun example, the competent arguer may elect to dramatize the two situations a bit, to sharpen the impression of dissimilarity: "I fail to see the analogy between walking home from a stalled car for one solid hour in a downpour and crossing thirty feet of grass in a sprinkle." (Bill Buckley's notorious [and notoriously effective] habit of listing his contentions by letters of the alphabet—"A, I didn't say that; B, if I had said it it would still not prove your point; and C, your illustration is irrelevant" is essentially a rhetorical device for making separate arguments—not always logically sequential—sound related in the specified sequence and [worse] as if they somehow led inexorably from one to the next.)

With regard to analogies, one must also remember, as already noted, to check whether the outcome in the allegedly analogous case really resulted from the cited similar facts, or from other circumstances, and whether the cited result was what your adversary claims it to have been.

The former pitfall is the natural habitat of the famous fallacy best known by its Latin formulation, *Post hoc ergo propter hoc* ("After this, therefore on account of this"). In other words, it is a familiar mistake to assume that just because one event followed another, the latter *necessarily* caused the former. "Farmer Jones retired when he was sixty-five, and was dead within two years"—or some variation thereof—is a familiar argument against the alleged perils of retirement. But of course the two facts are not necessarily related; Jones may have died of a stroke that had silently been building up in a cerebral artery for decades.

Ordinarily an arguer will take reasonable care to cite only analogies in which, however vulnerable the alleged factual similarities, the result, at least, fortifies his contention. But now and then even the result may be challenged as not being everything it is cracked up to be. That is the implicit point of the famous old pseudo-Victorian morality ode:

> *We never mention Aunt Clara;*
> *Her picture is turned to the wall.*
> *Though she lives on the French Riviera,*
> *Mother says she is dead to us all.*

Aunt Clara was clearly the family black sheep, and is held up by Mother as an awful example of the fate of the wicked. But the younger generation takes a rather different view of Clara's story, and concludes naughtily:

> *I shall live on the French Riviera*
> *And let Mother turn me to the wall!*

Similarly (in logical terms), is it so clear that many things we ordinarily consider desirable are invariably so? Money, for instance? Or length of life (without reference to its quality)? Wherever an argument is based on an analogy, it is at least worth inquiring into the actual outcome in the analogous case. For example, we are prone to think that the black Africans in the white-dominated states of southern Africa would naturally be better off if those areas were black-ruled; and if rule by one's own race, where that race dominates numerically, is indispensable to human dignity (as it may well be), the argument is logically unassailable. But the results in the nations to the north, where majority black rule has already succeeded minority white rule and are often cited as illustrations of the argument, are not very encouraging analogies when they are studied more closely. Many of them are military dictatorships; most of them are one-party states. The famous slogan "One man, one vote" has all too often been modified to the mocking counter: "One man, one vote, one time." The outcome in the analogous cases, in short, is undeniably vulnerable unless what makes people "better off" is carefully defined.

To sum up, then, an analogy is often useful, even if rarely decisive. Since it involves a set of (allegedly) parallel circumstances which led (allegedly) to a given (alleged) result, the attack can come at any of these three points by denying the similarity of the circumstances; by denying that they were the true cause of the result; or by denying that the result was in fact the one claimed. And don't forget: Several analogies are normally more persuasive than one.

MARSHALING THE FACTS: PREDICTING CONSEQUENCES

As we have seen, the argument by analogy often takes the form of a contention that a course of action being argued for (or against) will have certain desirable (or undesirable) consequences because, in a roughly similar situation, a similar course of action had those consequences. But it is possible to argue for or against a particular course of action on the basis of its probable consequences without resorting to an analogy to predict what those consequences will be.

In that case, the force of the argument derives solely from the intrinsic plausibility of the prediction, and that of course can range all the way from the overwhelming to the remote. One recent, much-bruited example of the genre was the so-called Domino Theory, propounded by those who favored U.S. military intervention in Southeast Asia. If South Vietnam were allowed to go down the drain (so this argument ran), the rest of the non-Communist nations in the region would succumb to Communism one after another, toppling like a row of dominoes: first Laos, then Cambodia, Thailand, Malaysia, Singapore, and Indonesia.

To proponents of the Domino Theory its logic seemed unassailable —even obvious. Opponents, however, took quite a different view, and countered the argument with considerable effect by conferring that subtly derisive sobriquet on it. They also persistently suggested (a planted axiom) that the Domino Theory had long since been exploded—even though this could not, of course, be done conclusively until and unless South Vietnam did in fact go down the drain and we could observe the geopolitical consequences.

(The postwar record of the Domino Theory is perhaps best described as "mixed." Laos was effectively taken over by its domestic Communists, aided by the North Vietnamese, as early as 1975. In that same year Cambodia was conquered by its pro-Communist Khmer Rouge forces. Subsequently, however, further Communist military expansion in the region has been blocked by quarrels among the Communist powers—an outcome that critics of the Domino Theory had long cited as likely. In particular, Peking and Hanoi have fallen out, and Vietnam [backed by the Soviet Union] in 1978 invaded Cambodia and replaced Pol Pot's pro-Chinese Communist regime with one equally Communist ,but subservient to itself and Moscow. But whether the toppling of the "dominoes" has ended or merely slowed remains to be seen. Certainly Peking's support for a Communist insurrection in Thailand has diminished—though Hanoi's intentions in that direction are ominously unclear. In any event, the ambiguous record of the Domino Theory to date illustrates both the strengths and weaknesses of an argument from consequences.)

One great virtue of the argument from consequences, strictly as a tactical matter, is that it cannot, almost by definition, be refuted conclusively while the argument is going on. A principle can sometimes be shown to be wholly inapplicable to a given situation. A fact can often be shown to be quite irrelevant—or, better yet, exploded as simply false. But a prediction can at best be criticized only as unlikely.

That was why I found the testimony of Rear Admiral Gene LaRocque (ret.) so frustrating, during a March 1974 "Advocates" program on whether the United States should end all military aid to South Vietnam regardless of the military situation on the ground there. (America's own military involvement had ended, of course, in 1973.) I was arguing against the proposal, defending roughly the administration's position that it was permitted under the Paris Accords to furnish Saigon with replacement materiel and that failure to do so would quickly result in the military collapse of South Vietnam. Admiral LaRocque, who had gone over to the "doves," was a witness for the other side. My "argument from consequences" was a flat prediction that, if we cut off military aid, South Vietnam was sure to collapse, since Moscow was actually stepping up its deliveries of military supplies to Hanoi. But Admiral LaRocque responded to my prediction by clinging stoutly to a quite different one of his own:

LAROCQUE: "I can't see a Communist takeover of a nation of eighteen million people who have fought valiantly for all of these years to preserve their own integrity as a nation. I don't see it as even a possibility—couldn't even speculate on it."

RUSHER: "Whether they have weapons or not?"

LAROCQUE: "The people of South Vietnam were fighting the North long before we came. They'll be fighting the North long after we leave, and the level of fighting and the type of fighting will probably change as we reduce our military support to South Vietnam."

RUSHER: "What if I told you—or suggested to you—that American military and economic support to the Thieu government is absolutely crucial to prevent its collapse?"

LAROCQUE: "I wouldn't buy it."

And there we stood—at loggerheads. It was left to the audience, as it had to be, to decide for itself which scenario was the more plausible.

As this illustration demonstrates, the effectiveness of an argument from consequences is far more dependent on the perceptions of the target audience than (for example) an argument based upon an objective fact, or even upon a principle—which, like a fact, may have weight with an audience if it is recognized, whether the audience is happy with its application or not. A prediction has weight only to the extent that it is credited, and the degree of credit it receives is often, perhaps even generally, related to the predispositions of the target audience. In the particular instance just cited, a majority of the PBS television audience was strongly opposed to further U.S. participation, even by means of supply only, in the Vietnamese war. (I lost the audience vote, 68 percent to 32 percent.) I do not suggest that Admiral LaRocque's expectations were shared by most of those who sided with him against me, but it seems likely that his prediction was accorded more weight than it deserved because a majority of the audience was predisposed in his favor.

(For my fellow "hawks," of course, LaRocque's prediction probably had a reinforcing effect in my favor: It was so wildly at odds with what seemed to us the inevitable outcome that it damaged the force of his over-all position. If, by 1974, there were any true neutrals left out there in the audience, it may have had a similar effect on them. Certainly I hoped so.)

The argument from consequences, then, tends on the whole to be somewhat weaker than the argument from analogy (which, as we have seen, is essentially a subdivision of it), precisely because it lacks the stiffening of plausibility which a reasonably apposite analogy provides. The prediction has to fly on its own, as it were; and it flies, or falls, depending on the target audience's (often biased) perception of its likelihood.

IX

RHETORICAL DEVICES

Thus far we have discussed the basic substantive techniques of argumentation: appealing to principles and marshaling facts, including under the latter the prediction of consequences either with the support of an analogy or without it. We will now turn to various techniques that have less to do with the *sort* of material presented than with the *way in which* it is presented. These are often called "rhetorical devices," and they have in some quarters a lower reputation than the "pure" forms of argumentation because they involve considerations that are other than strictly intellectual. They concern themselves, in other words, not merely with whether an argument (or a counter to one) is "good"—i.e., objectively effective—but with how to put it forward in a way that will *maximize* its effectiveness.

Those who oppose, theoretically, the use of such rhetorical devices seem to me to be living in a dream world. No doubt an argument ought to be, at bottom, a rational exchange of views in which one view is at length demonstrated to be superior. But only a Utopian could envision such an exchange being conducted wholly without resort to rhetorical devices. In the first place, such rhetorical touches as anger, incredulity, and humor often serve as a sort of shorthand to communicate a point of view that might otherwise require lengthy explication. Even short of that, they are frequently used to indicate the tone or degree of emphasis the speaker wishes to place on a point —rather like accent marks in certain foreign languages. The mother who tells her child to "Come here" is conveying her desire unemotionally. When she tells the child, "I said, 'Come *here*'" she is indulging in a rhetorical device (in fact, two of them), and the effectiveness of the instruction is heightened accordingly.

Beyond such merely diacritical uses, however, rhetorical devices can enhance the effectiveness of an argument by involving our emotions in it. This is, to be sure, a violation of the purely rational aspects of argumentation but is improper only to the extent that emotional grace-notes are inappropriate. I doubt, for example, that many people would object, even on grounds of pure theory, to the injection of a refreshing note of sheer humor into a discussion that is threatening to become too dryly rational. And stronger emotions—e.g., pity or anger—can surely be invoked when "the heart has its reasons." We are not totally rational beings, and the art of verbal communication is only some fifty thousand years old. No wonder, then, that the most successful communicators (and hence arguers) have always availed themselves of means of communication that antedate the twenty-six letters of the English alphabet.

ASKING A QUESTION

Let us begin with a rhetorical device that isn't even a "device" unless its purpose is designedly rhetorical: i.e., asking a question. A question may naturally be asked, in the course of an argument, solely for the purpose of information ("What do you mean when you say 'conservative'?"), or to narrow a loose contention ("Are you saying it would be wrong, or merely that it would be indiscreet?"). But many a question is asked in an argument not to elicit information or to clarify a contention, but in order to force some answer—usually one unserviceable to the person being questioned. These are designed, not to produce new information, but to illuminate some already-chosen point, and they are called "rhetorical questions."

We have already discussed rhetorical questions as a means of discountenancing the factual expertise of "experts," or the assertions of factual testimony in general. More broadly, the rule we cited for cross-examinations holds true, and obedience to it results in questions that are in the strictest sense rhetorical: Never ask a question to which you do not know, and cannot compel, the answer.

A relatively simple example of such a question is the one I asked a hostile witness on a January 1974 "Advocates" program concerning nuclear power. As usual, and quite properly, the opposition was stressing the danger of accidents at nuclear facilities. Knowing that, in the case of one particularly horrendous accident, no deleterious effects had (at least yet) been identified, I moved to nail down the point with a rhetorical question that fulfilled both of the classical requirements: I knew the answer, and could—in theory—compel it, though the witness (Professor Henry Kendall of M.I.T.) did his best to leave open the possibility of future adverse effects as yet unperceived:

RUSHER: "With regard to radioactive waste, we heard about the 150,000 gallons of radioactive waste that was leaked not long ago out of that tank in Hanford [Oregon]—not a commercial plant to be sure, but nonetheless radioactive waste that was leaked out into the ground. What happened as a result of that leak?"

KENDALL: "Well, we don't know what will happen—"

RUSHER: "No, that's not what I asked, Dr. Kendall. What *happened*? I'm no longer, for the moment, if you don't mind, interested in your speculations as to what *may*, or what you don't know may. What *happened*?"

KENDALL: "What happened was a great concern about atomic energy practices in dealing with radioactive waste. That's the first thing."

RUSHER: "What else?"

KENDALL: "An inspection of the bad procedures that led to those leaks."

RUSHER: "Right."

KENDALL: "Not only corroding tanks, but new equipment which failed."

RUSHER: "Did anything else happen?"

KENDALL: "Well, I'm not certain what you mean. There has been a detailed investigation—"

RUSHER: "Come on! If we have 150,000 gallons of radioactive waste spilling out onto the ground, I would assume, on the basis of the testimony that you have given and that Mr. Cherry has alluded to here, that something would happen, something negative, something undesirable."

KENDALL: "Mr. Rusher, these are insidious materials and the potential is there for devastating difficulties in the future—"

RUSHER: "I know the 'potential' is there—"

KENDALL: "—and it is no way to run the program, to have these—"

RUSHER: "May I assume that your answer is that nothing happened?"

KENDALL: "You may not."

RUSHER: "It was like the Sherlock Holmes dog that didn't bark in the nighttime."

Besides forcing a hostile witness to testify to facts you know and can compel him to corroborate, rhetorical questions can be used to diminish the credibility of a witness (even an expert) if you are fortunate enough to possess evidence that he once took a position different from that for which he is now contending. Such contretemps are among the most delicious in the whole field of argumentation, and audiences naturally enjoy them immoderately since they discomfit the person questioned right before their eyes.

That was the bind in which I prepared to squeeze Professor Allan Goodman of Clark University, when he appeared with Admiral LaRocque on that 1974 "Advocates" program concerning whether we should end all military aid to South Vietnam. My research staff had discovered that in May 1973, just ten months before the broadcast, Professor Goodman had asserted, in writing, that "American military and economic aid to the Thieu Government is absolutely crucial to prevent its collapse." Now he had changed his mind, and I proposed to tax him with his inconsistency. He was, of course, prepared at least for the possibility that I was aware of his earlier statement, and when I brought it up he moved to counteract its effect by a display of high confidence:

RUSHER: "You stated in May of 1973—and I'm most anxious to have you elucidate the statement—"

GOODMAN: "Great."

RUSHER: "—and I quote, that 'American military and economic'— *military and* economic—'support to the Thieu Government is absolutely crucial to prevent its collapse.' Is that true?"

GOODMAN: "That is exactly what I stated in May of 1973, and the reason I'm here—"

RUSHER: "Correct."

GOODMAN: "—the reason I'm here—"

RUSHER: "Yes?"

GOODMAN: "—the reason that I'm here is that I've come to reevaluate that."

To which I replied dryly:

RUSHER: "You've changed your mind."

GOODMAN: "I had no idea, and I don't think the American people have any idea, of the amount of aid we've given to Saigon in the past eighteen months."

RUSHER: "So everything you said in May of last year is wrong, about this particular point?"

GOODMAN: "What I said in May last year was that the future of South Vietnam would be determined by political competition."

RUSHER: "Well, that's not, I think, in part, what you said."

GOODMAN: "What I said last year—"

RUSHER: "If I may quote exactly what you said, 'American military and economic support to the Thieu Government is absolutely crucial.'"

GOODMAN: "Yes."

RUSHER: "That was wrong?"

GOODMAN: "Yes, and I admit it."

RUSHER: "Why was it wrong?"

GOODMAN: "Because the fundamental problem that Thieu faces today is political and economic."

RUSHER: "Was it then?"

GOODMAN: "No, I wasn't sure what it was then."

RUSHER: "You weren't sure. Are you sure now?"

GOODMAN: "Yes, I am."

RUSHER: "So now that you've changed your mind, you're right?"

GOODMAN: "No more than any of us are right."

RUSHER: "Exactly. We're all right and wrong, so it doesn't matter. But in any case, you were wrong?"

GOODMAN: "That's right."

Bad as it was, Goodman at least knew he had made the statement in question. Far worse was the position of William A. Henry III, a Boston television columnist who appeared on an "Advocates" program in April 1979 in support of a larger federal subsidy for the Public Broadcasting System (as recommended by the second Carnegie

Commission). This time my researchers had discovered no less than two comments in Mr. Henry's voluminous column output that were implicitly critical of PBS' use of federal money. As the advocate on the negative side of the proposal, I laid a trap for him:

RUSHER: "Would you agree with the statement that 'In practice, public television seeks public money without accountability?'"

HENRY: "No, I don't think so. I—"

RUSHER: "Why did you make it, then? I've been studying you. I'm quoting you, Mr. Henry."

Henry, however, managed to struggle more or less clear of the implicit charge of inconsistency by distinguishing the context of the quoted statement:

HENRY: "What I said was, 'No one but the system's own employees lobbies for quality television, for an artistic vision that ignores ratings and special interests.'"

RUSHER: "Let me read you this—"

HENRY: "'That vision sounds elitist and in practice, it seeks public money without accountability—'"

RUSHER: "'Seeks public money without accountability—'"

HENRY: "That is, that some employees in the public television system want to do only high art."

So far, so good, but Mr. Henry, perhaps misled by his partial success in avoiding my first trap, promptly fell into a second:

RUSHER: "Would it—would it be fair to say that before asking for more money, public broadcasting should do a better job with the money it has? You know, it has been said that 'Its office is on the sweeping sixth floor of the building in the Mussolini-monumental new L'Enfant Plaza in Washington.' You know who said that, don't you?"

HENRY: "I'm not sure that I do."

RUSHER: "You did. Another one of those— You should read your columns more often."

HENRY: "I write eight of them a week. I can't always appreciate—"

RUSHER: "Yes, I suppose."

HENRY: "—when a clever phrase is my own."

A reasonably suave comeback, but no great help to Mr. Henry's over-all reputation for consistency.

Inconsistency, by the way, is no respecter of persons. In 1949 the great Winston Churchill was deftly pinked by then-Prime Minister Clement Attlee for opposing a government bill to limit further the power of the House of Lords, although Churchill himself in 1911 (as a member of Asquith's Liberal government) had favored an earlier proposal in the same direction. Attlee delightedly quoted some rolling periods of the younger Churchill's, denouncing the House of Lords as "hereditary, irresponsible, unrepresentative, absentee." Churchill, in reply, could only object good-naturedly that his long service in Parliament (by then already stretching over nearly half a century) ought to be taken into account and give rise to some sort of Statute of Limitations. He was, Churchill said, prepared to be held accountable for everything he had said for thirty years past; beyond that, he felt, a charitable veil ought to be drawn over his utterances. Few of us, fortunately in this case, ever live long enough to be caught in a contradiction over such a period of time.

There is one large subdivision of the general subject of questioning a hostile witness in which the cards are stacked so thoroughly against the questioner as to render the whole process of asking a question inadvisable. This is where one is invited to ask a question of a public speaker. In such cases, the speaker is, in effect, a hostile witness, since the implicit objective of the questioner—unless (*per impossibile*, as Bill Buckley would say) he merely seeks enlightenment—is to ask a question that will force the speaker to modify or at least spell out his position or otherwise make some concession.

The difficulties of such a format are, from the standpoint of the questioner, so numerous as to be, almost always, fatal. I have been on both sides of that fence, and I know. The central difficulty is that the person questioned practically always has the last word—no small advantage, as we have already seen. Even if the questioner is allowed a "follow-up question," the person he is questioning automatically gets a "follow-up answer"—and, again, the last word.

The difficulties are compounded by the fact that the format requires the questioner to put a *question*, rather than employ any other form of statement. For while just about any point can be put in the form of a question ("Isn't it true that . . ."), the questioner is necessarily cast in the role of a person seeking enlightenment, while the person questioned enjoys the role of someone grandly dispensing it. All in all, a most unsatisfactory posture for the questioner.

We see this tableau in full flower in the presidential press conference—an institution reporters regard as almost sacred, yet which is often deeply frustrating to them. The Chief Executive arrives in grandeur; everyone must rise when he enters the room. He graciously bids them be seated, makes an announcement or two, then recognizes the AP or UPI White House correspondent to ask the first question. White House correspondents are a tough and able bunch, and the President is well and truly quizzed; but the high cards are all still in his hands. He can recognize one reporter and disregard another; he can make an answer as long or short, humorous or serious, as he wishes; he can allow a "follow-up question" or immediately recognize another reporter interested in a wholly different subject; etc., etc. In about thirty minutes the senior wire service reporter's "Thank you, Mr. President" will bring the press conference to a close, no matter how many questions remain unasked (or unanswered).

Indeed, the disabilities of a mere questioner are so numerous and so profound that I ordinarily refuse to play the role at all. Once, however, many years ago, I managed to confect a highly satisfactory rhetorical question that stopped an accomplished speaker right in his tracks.

The year, if I recall correctly, was 1953, squarely in the midst of the great controversy over the Red-hunting tactics of Senator Joseph McCarthy. The New York Young Republican Club, a largely liberal group of Young Republicans, had invited Brigadier General Telford Taylor to address its "downtown luncheon," held regularly at Schwartz's Restaurant in the Wall Street area. Taylor, who was a liberal Democrat, made various slyly humorous references to "*your* party," and for some reason elected to patronize Senator McCarthy as having behaved somewhat better in recent months—"rather like the boy at camp who got the medal for having 'improved most' during the summer." When he had suavely concluded his speech and the chairman called for questions, I rose and said:

"General Taylor, we have all enjoyed your witty remarks on the vicissitudes of 'our party,' and the medal you evidently feel Senator

McCarthy has earned for his recent behavior. To keep the record in balance, though, I thought it would be well to recall that the last time *your* party was in power the Director of the Office of Special Political Affairs of the Department of State [Alger Hiss] was a Russian spy, and the Deputy Chief of the Presentation Division of the Office of Strategic Services [Carl Aldo Marzani] was a secret Communist, and the secretary of the National Labor Relations Board [Nathan Witt] was a secret Communist. And I was just wondering, General, what medals you are handing out for that performance, and whether you have anything witty to say about it?"

Taylor (a New York attorney who had earned his brigadier-general's rank as an Army prosecutor of war criminals) leaned back against a blackboard behind him, lowered his eyelids to half-mast, and replied, "That question is not germane to my topic today."

Even where the protagonists are on a theoretical par, care must always be taken that the question asked does not merely afford one's adversary an opportunity to hog the limelight and restate his own case. I still recall as one of the most frustrating evenings of my life the occasion on which I participated in a panel with Bella Abzug, then congressperson from Manhattan's West Side. I had at first declined to do so, on the ground that Mrs. Abzug would overwhelm the proceedings with her well-known leather lungs and powerful personality. I was assured that the panel chairman would firmly gavel Mrs. Abzug down if she overstepped her time limits or other restraints; and besides our fellow panelists would be Herb Klein (the knowledgeable and likable former Nixon press aide) and Av Westin, executive producer of ABC News—both wise and worldly men. So finally I agreed to participate.

The proceedings at the New York Hilton were to be videotaped at 8 P.M. sharp (for subsequent TV broadcast) before a crowd of perhaps two hundred, who as it turned out were largely Abzug supporters on hand to cheer their heroine. Mrs. Abzug was late, and after waiting about twenty minutes the chairman finally started the proceedings without her, calling on one of my fellow panelists to make an opening statement. About halfway through this Mrs. Abzug could be heard arriving, and when she entered the room and clumped up onto the stage her fans broke into a tumultuous welcome that lasted (while she waved back at them) several minutes.

When order had finally been restored the opening speaker resumed, more or less, the trampled thread of his discourse. Then the rest of us spoke, one at a time, including Mrs. Abzug—she much longer than the rest. Clearly, despite the assurances I had been given, the chairman was not going to be able to discipline her. What ruined the evening for me, however, was the behavior of Messrs. Klein and Westin when the chairman finally did wrest the floor from Mrs. Abzug and recognize first one and then the other of them. So help me, *both* of these kind and sensible men said, "I would like to ask Mrs. Abzug how she can say" thus and so. Mrs. Abzug in both cases promptly resumed the floor and treated us to another twenty minutes of her oratory, explaining precisely how she could say thus and so.

I walked home that evening, from the Hilton to Murray Hill, and still had to take a Miltown to get to sleep. A week later my dentist told me my teeth showed distinct signs of recent grinding!

Questions then, if asked at all, should be shaped as far as possible to compel a desirable response, or at the very least avoid an undesirable one. If this is impossible, they are probably best avoided altogether. More than once during my years on "The Advocates," and especially in fields of knowledge when I myself felt insecure (e.g., the arcana of economics), somebody would urge me to ask a particular question of a hostile witness. "Ask him such-and-such," my adviser would counsel me, "and he'll *have* to say thus-and-so. Then you can zap him with XYZ." It sounded like the perfect cross-exam question: One to which I knew, and could compel, the answer. But I was only taking some friend's word for it that the witness would "have to say" thus-and-so. More often than not, when I rose to put the question, he would say something quite different. Which always reminded me of the parody:

> The boy stood on the burning deck,
> And all about was air.
> Then some damned fool removed the deck
> And left him standing there!

OTHER RHETORICAL DEVICES

We have already noted how humor, pity, or even anger can be used to maximize the effect of a point. The same may be said of a display of almost any other human emotion or behavior—courtesy, incredulity, certitude, sympathy, impatience, indifference, scorn, surprise. In this way a skillful arguer can often lead his target audience along some preselected path of carefully chosen emotions: a courteous, low-keyed beginning; the quickening pace that verges on impatience with a sluggish response; the heightened surprise at a (theoretically) unexpected answer; the ensuing incredulity, slowly hardening into scorn. Or whatever.

There is simply no denying the impact of such devices when they are skillfully employed. Those who heard it assure me that the rhetorical high-point of John Henry Faulk's libel suit against Vincent Hartnett and the anti-Communist organization Aware was the moment when Louis Nizer, Faulk's attorney, thought (or professed to think) his own patriotism had come under implicit attack by one of Hartnett's lawyers. In the presence of the jury, Nizer—a man of imposing personal presence—turned on his critic with majestic scorn: "How *dare* you, sir? How *dare* you!" The jury subsequently awarded Faulk a 3-million-dollar verdict—which may or may not be a case of *post hoc ergo propter hoc.*

But courtrooms, while famous as the scene of such displays of emotion, aren't their only venue. A board room, or a family's breakfast table, will often do as well. Wherever human beings communicate, we can expect all forms of communication.

Just one step beyond communication by means of emotional displays is communication by means of physical displays: i.e., Body English. The two forms of communication actually overlap: A skillful arguer will in part communicate a relaxed and accepting mood by a given physical posture, and convey an angry or scornful one with the help of quite a different one.

There is one physical display that is so effective in comparison with its merely intellectual or emotional equivalents, that it deserves separate and special mention, and that is eye contact. I don't know which participant in some aboriginal High Noon first discovered the persuasive impact of looking directly and persistently into the other person's eyes, but there is no doubt whatever about the effectiveness of the tactic. Of course, looking firmly into another person's eyes may be downright intimidating, but it needn't necessarily be so: Eye contact can, under the right circumstances, suggest openness, innocence, simplicity, nothing-to-hide. It can also challenge another person (e.g., to tell the whole truth), or even simply hold his attention. Whichever way it is used, it is generally quite effective.

Conversely, an unwillingness or inability to look another person in the eye is usually a serious disadvantage. It connotes the negative of all the qualities mentioned above: deviousness, guilt; at a minimum, uncertainty. I know a politician—a professional campaign manager—who for whatever reason is simply incapable of looking anyone in the eye. Instead, he looks fixedly at a point slightly inshore from the left shoulder of the person he is addressing. This has almost, but not quite, the same effect as using a teleprompter, which a TV newscaster can look at and read from while the viewer has the distinct impression that the newscaster is looking him straight in the eye. This particular politician, however, winds up leaving his listeners subliminally unsure whether he is crooked or merely walleyed.

Another rhetorical device largely dependent upon physical manifestations—or rather, in this case, the lack of them—is the conveying of indifference. In any public context an arguer is always "onstage," so to speak, and the audience will be quick to notice if he is surprised or (worse yet) stung by any point his opponent makes.

Some years ago the Sunday New York *Times Magazine*, in the course of an article about trial attorneys, quoted a lawyer in a large Wall Street firm, who did *not* engage in trial practice, as pitying (but also admiring) those of his partners who did: "You have to have the stamina of a dray horse," he said. "You also have to sit there looking cool and on top of everything while somebody is surprising the hell out of you." In a sense, indifference is an emotion like any other, and it too can be communicated physically.

Turning to rhetorical devices less dependent on physical actions, how about the oldest of them all: the direct appeal to emotion? As the reader may by now anticipate, I have no overarching objection to it. Inevitably, everybody indulges in it to some degree; the words we all must use are seldom absolutely neutral emotionally. It is really only a question of the relevance of the emotion invoked to the particular point under discussion. A neat bilateral example of this occurred in the aforementioned "Advocates" program on whether the death penalty should be restored. Dr. Louis J. West, a California psychiatrist appearing for the negative, explained under questioning by Professor Alan Dershowitz that he had come to oppose the death penalty as a result of the painful experience of serving as the attending physician at an execution:

WEST: "I went through World War II and medical school and psychiatric training and was perfectly content with the death penalty. And then, on one day in August of 1952, I participated in an execution in Iowa. We hanged a fellow there for murder. And as medical examiner, I stood at the end of a rope and listened to his heart slow down and stop. It took about twelve and a half minutes. That converted me to a student of this problem, and I've studied it carefully for twenty years, and I'm now absolutely opposed to the death penalty for any reason."

A pretty grisly description—and a very effective one. On cross-examination I moved quickly to counter the image with a still more horrifying one that tended to tip the scales in the opposite direction:

RUSHER: "I can sympathize with your feelings as you watched an execution. Were you, by any chance, the medical examiner who examined the bodies of Sharon Tate and Charlie Manson's other four victims?"

WEST: "No, sir."

RUSHER: "You will recall that Sharon Tate was pregnant and that, I think, all of the victims had some thirty or forty stab wounds in them?"

WEST: "Gruesome murders, indeed."

RUSHER: "Would you consider the gruesomeness of that spectacle a logical argument in favor of the death penalty?"

WEST: "No, not a bit."

RUSHER (angrily): "Well, then, why do you consider the difficulties that you observed when a man was hanging as a logical argument *against* it?"

WEST: "I didn't say it was a logical argument."

RUSHER: "Why did you use it?"

WEST: "I used it as a description of the onset of my study of this, which was based upon me as a physician participating in a procedure when a helpless captive was exterminated."

RUSHER: "I suggest to you that you used it as an emotional device. Or perhaps Professor Dershowitz suggested that you do so."

WEST: "Until you've been at a hanging, sir, don't put down the emotionality of it."

RUSHER: "I'm not putting down the emotionality of it—nor of the crimes that were committed by Mr. Manson."

Now, the point here is that both Dr. West and I were appealing to the emotions of the viewers: he, by describing the clinical details of a hanging; I, by describing the even more gruesome details of a particularly vicious multiple murder. Perhaps a more fastidious arguer would feel that both devices were cheap shots: Everyone is aware that condemned men die; everyone is aware that murder victims are often killed in horrible ways. But personally I felt, and still feel, that both of these appeals to the audience's emotions were justified. One of the arguments against the death penalty is precisely the horror of the state's cold-blooded termination of a human life. And one of the arguments in favor of the death penalty is a timely reminder of the terrible deed it avenges. The fact that these highly relevant reflections stir our emotions is not an argument against them, it seems to me, but in their favor.

On the other hand, an appeal may of course be made to some emotion that is entirely, or almost entirely, irrelevant to the issue at hand. Edward J. Reilly, Bruno Hauptmann's attorney in his trial for kidnaping the Lindbergh baby, was a notorious old demagogue who thought nothing of whipping a small American flag out of his pocket during his final speech to the jurors to suggest that their patriotic instincts ought to sway them in his client's favor. In the circumstances, that was going pretty far.

But what about my own practice, during 1970 and 1971, of wearing a small American-flag lapel pin? A number of "Advocates" viewers, noticing it, took offense. Was I, as they charged, subtly suggesting that my opponent's side of the various debates we engaged in was somehow unpatriotic?

First let me emphasize that I wore the pin regularly in those years —not merely on "Advocates" programs. The country was deeply divided at that time on a whole series of issues relating to the Vietnam war. Opponents of the war were engaging in a large number of forms of "symbolic speech," such as burning their draft cards, carrying mock coffins around the White House, etc. In a broader sense the entire "counterculture" proclaimed itself by the clothes it wore, the beards and hair-do's it sported, etc. It seemed to me and many other people that wearing an American-flag lapel pin was a way of signaling our own contrary view on a whole series of issues without having to wear a sandwich board. It was not, in my own case, intended as a comment on any particular issue that was debated on "The Advocates"—though it undeniably served to summarize my world view in general.

Finally, what about those twin rhetorical devices, overstatement and understatement? Both have the same purpose: to stress a point. Overstatement accomplishes this by exaggerating it. Understatement achieves the same end more subtly, by deliberately diminishing the point and leaving it to the audience to correct the imbalance by enlarging the point to its legitimate proportions.

A particularly delicious example of the latter that I have always treasured was Winston Churchill's mild remark in the House of Commons in 1940 concerning Nazi Germany's exaggerated claims as to the number of British planes that were being shot down in the Battle of Britain. Churchill, who reveled in publicly referring to Hitler as "this bloodthirsty guttersnipe" (among many other endearments), could have made the rafters ring with some vivid denunciation of the unparalleled depths of Hitler's mendacity. Instead, he pretended to worry about the German dictator's good name: "If Herr Hitler does not cease these misrepresentations," he warned, "his reputation for veracity may be impugned." The fastidious choice of words with Latin roots underscored the mock delicacy of the statement.

Which is better: overstatement or understatement? Many people will answer at once: understatement. And this is generally true wherever overstatement might lead an audience to feel that it was being manipulated. In such a case the audience will tend to overcorrect for the overstated point, leaving it valued less than it was in the begin-

ning, or (perhaps) than it deserves to be. What's more, the audience
may conclude that if an arguer overstates his case in an instance of
which they are aware, he is probably also overstating it in instances
of which they are *not* aware—i.e., is deceiving them right across the
board. The dangers here are obvious.

In general, then, it will often be desirable to understate one's
point slightly, *provided* it is clear to the audience that it *is* being un-
derstated and the audience can be depended on to enhance it appro-
priately themselves. They will credit the arguer with a scrupulous
concern not to exaggerate, and like him the better for it.

But this would be a poorer world without overstatement, and it
has—despite everything just said about its dangers—a valid place in
argumentation. Provided, above all, that the audience recognizes the
exaggeration as deliberate but not malignant—i.e., not intended to
deceive—it can highlight a point without injuring it in the least. Listen to the deft way in which Robert E. Crowe, the prosecutor in the
famous Leopold and Loeb murder case, alluded to his great adversary, defense attorney Clarence Darrow, in his summation to the
judge who had tried the case without a jury: "The distinguished gentleman concerning whose health thieves inquire before they go to
commit a crime . . ."

An exaggeration, of course. But so extreme that the judge well
knew he was not expected to take the charge literally. He was, rather,
being gently reminded that Mr. Darrow had been many a felon's
passport to the great outdoors; and no doubt he accepted the point
as thus lightly made.*

As a matter of fact, most great oratory and most advocacy litera-
ture indulges, with our permission and even our gratitude, in a certain amount of overstatement. Not all: The speeches of Lincoln, in
particular, seem to avoid it conscientiously—as if Lincoln sensed that
the problems he addressed were too profound and too precariously
balanced to permit of the slightest exaggeration. The Gettysburg
Address, to take just one example, is as devoid of overstatement
(though not, and rightly not, of generalization) as it is possible for a
speech to be. It achieves its whole tremendous impact by understatement—by a sort of rhetorical jujitsu, in fact, in which the very

* It did not, of course, ultimately deter him from sentencing Leopold and Loeb
to life in prison, as Darrow urged, rather than to death.

momentousness of the issues discussed is forced to lend its weight to the spare construction and lean words that Lincoln used.

But who can help rejoicing at Winston Churchill's whole-souled denunciation of St. John (Lord Bolingbroke), the great enemy of his ancestor John Churchill, in his impassioned biography of the latter? He has traced St. John's devious path through eighteenth-century British politics in detail, and now in a single overpowering sentence he sums it up. We may sense that we are reading something more like a lawyer's brief than a historian's balanced judgment, but how we love it!—

> By personal vices of heart and mind, by deeds of basest treachery, by violation of law and public faith, this man St. John—unpurposed, unprincipled, miscreant adventurer—had brought his native land to the edge of the abyss; and in this horrid juncture he could not even clothe crime with coherency.

We quiver with awe at the evil man Churchill depicts, even if we have never heard of St. John before. We instinctively *hope* he is as guilty as Churchill so superbly says he is—and that is one of overstatement's highest (and, to be sure, most dangerous) contributions to the art of argumentation.

To sum up, then: Rhetorical devices are nothing to be ashamed of. On the contrary, they are indispensable tools serving as they do to enhance and enrich the plodding words that necessarily form the basic substance of human communication. They are only unfair—and if so perceived, dangerous to the user—when those in the audience feel they are being used manipulatively. An audience, in other words—even an audience of one—enjoys being entertained, but dislikes being deceived. The competent arguer, remembering this, takes care to convince the audience that he has nothing up his sleeves. Once assured on that point, the audience will be quite willing—indeed eager—to watch his show indulgently.

WHEN ALL ELSE FAILS

Before leaving the matter of rhetorical devices altogether, let us note a category of them that is occasionally employed by masters of the blacker arts of argumentation to interrupt some booming contention of an adversary's that threatens to become altogether too effective.

You know the type of situation I mean. The adversary has some good point and is in the process of making it in some particularly effective and rather lengthy way: a long Ciceronian periodic sentence perhaps, or a staccato series of barked questions. Older readers may remember Stephen Potter, the British comic writer of the 1950s who invented the art of "gamesmanship"—a series of hilarious "ploys," all devised for use on various tedious experts and all designed to *"break the stupefying flow"* (Potter's italics). That sums up precisely the objective of the rhetorical devices I am about to describe.

One has come to be filed in my memory under the title "the Buckley *glissando.*" I heard Bill use it during a radio debate about twenty years ago on the late George Hamilton Combs.

Combs was one of the most formidable debaters I have ever encountered. He was the son of an ordained minister and had served as a Democratic Congressman from Missouri, then moved to New York to become (among other things) a commentator for radio station WOR and vice chairman of the speakers' bureau of the Democratic National Committee. In addition to all else, nature had endowed him with a fine deep voice of the type sometimes called a "beer baritone." As A. E. Housman wrote in another connection, he was "weapon'd and accouter'd well / From the arsenals of Hell."

On the occasion in question Combs was zestily pursuing some pungent point down the home stretch of a magnificent sentence when one became aware of a high, thin "Oh" sound that floated above Combs' rolling barrage and descended slowly with it, rather like Norma's *glissando* above the chorus of the Druid priests in *Casta diva.* Syntactically, Buckley's "Oh" was nothing more than the first word of some such sentence as "Oh come now, Mr. Combs," launched a bit too soon and simply maintained until Combs was through. But the effect was devastating. The ear was irretrievably captured by that high, descending "Oh"—nobody who heard it could possibly pay the slightest attention to whatever Combs was saying so majestically.

Which, just possibly, was Buckley's idea.

Perhaps Combs learned from the experience, or perhaps he had known the trick all along, because years later, when he and I were pairing off on a justifiably short-lived program on WOR called "Let's Take Sides," Combs successfully used a variant of the same tactic on me. This time I was the one with the long, thunderous sentence rolling out of my mouth, my attention fixed on a crushing verb some two or three dependent clauses away, when Combs suddenly began to bark "Come, come!" Just that, brusquely, over and over again: "Come, come! Come, come! Come, come! Come, come!" I finished the sentence, but I knew no one had heard it. It was like trying to play a violin while descending the Khumbu Ice Fall below Mt. Everest.

A simpler and to my mind less satisfactory variant of the same technique is merely to tell an adversary who is doing you harm to "Come off it." This is roughly the arguer's equivalent of a boxer going into a clinch; it accomplishes nothing affirmative, but at least temporarily ends the punishment. Once several years ago I was invited to a large cocktail party which in due course evolved into a sit-down dinner at some four or five tables of ten each. The seating had looked casual—in fact, entirely coincidental—but a woman at my table quickly engaged me in a political argument and I gradually realized she had planned to sit at my table and get even for various wounds I had unwittingly inflicted on her, via TV and radio, over the years. It transpired that she had been the Democratic mayor of a small suburban town, and was a highly competent arguer of the liberal persuasion. Slowly I became interested, then intent, and finally obsessed; everybody at the table was listening, some with quite justified embarrassment, but I plowed on and finally, getting the lady over some logical barrel or other, demanded that she answer my question. She couldn't; instead, "Come off it, Mr. Rusher." I asked the question again. "Come off it." Question. "Come off it." Question. "Come off it." Finally, with the help of the others, I changed the subject. What else was there to do?

Such rhetorical devices are not recommended here—certainly not the last one. But every competent arguer ought to be aware that they exist, for he may meet one of them on the road some day. If so, he has my sympathy!

X

BLUNDERS

WHEN YOU MAKE A MISTAKE

No matter how competent an arguer may be, the time will inevitably come when he makes a mistake. It may be big or small, crucial or inconsequential, but we are all human and to err is human. Fortunately, the rule for dealing with this sort of situation is well established and almost makes up, in its simplicity, for its undeniable painfulness. It is: *Back away*, quickly and completely. Do it unostentatiously if possible, but above all do it. No matter how disagreeable the immediate effect of such a retreat may be, it is infinitely preferable to trying to defend a position that one knows, deep down, is indefensible against an adversary who usually knows it as well as you do.

A classic illustration of this point was President Ford's remark concerning Poland in his second campaign debate with Mr. Carter on October 6, 1976. In responding to a question by New York *Times* reporter Max Frankel, a member of the panel, Ford inadvertently let himself be understood as saying that Poland was not dominated by the Soviet Union—which was of course absurd, since its government is in fact a one-party Communist dictatorship sustained by Russian bayonets. Here were Mr. Ford's exact words:

"And what has been accomplished by the Helsinki Agreement? No. 1, we have an agreement where they notify us and we notify them of any military maneuvers that are to be undertaken. They have done it. In both cases where they've done so, there is no Soviet domination of Eastern Europe and there never will be under a Ford Administration."

Frankel promptly moved to give Ford an opportunity to correct his error:

"I'm sorry, could I just follow—did I understand you to say, sir, that the Russians are not using Eastern Europe as their own sphere of influence in occupying most of the countries there and making sure with their troops that it's a Communist zone?"

But apparently Ford had been advised by his managers not under any circumstances to show anything that might be interpreted as uncertainty or indecisiveness. Or perhaps he just sensed that it isn't a plus for a Chief Executive to have to correct his own mistake in front of 83 million television viewers. Whatever his reason, Ford elected to deny that he had misspoken or been mistaken:

"I don't believe, Mr. Frankel, that the Yugoslavians consider themselves dominated by the Soviet Union. I don't believe that the Rumanians consider themselves dominated by the Soviet Union. I don't believe that the Poles consider themselves dominated by the Soviet Union.

"Each of those countries is independent, autonomous, it has its own territorial integrity, and the United States does not concede that those countries are under the domination of the Soviet Union. As a matter of fact, I visited Poland, Yugoslavia, and Rumania to make certain that the people of those countries understood that the President of the United States and the people of the United States are dedicated to their independence, their autonomy and their freedom."

Now, it clearly won't do to suggest that an incumbent President of the United States just didn't know that Poland today is Soviet-dominated. Mr. Ford was simply making the classical error of throwing good money after bad—trying to retrieve a mistake by denying, somehow, that it was one. Perhaps he made a hard-eyed estimate that, among the 83 million in the audience, the vast majority would be favorably impressed by his sheer certitude and wouldn't realize he was wrong. (Perhaps, even, he was right about that.)

But Mr. Ford had blundered all the same, and in the ensuing days and weeks before the election he paid dearly for it. Practically every column and editorial written about that debate mentioned his mistake, and wondered aloud whether he was really stupid or just mulishly stubborn. It wasn't a happy choice to offer the voters. Carter kept the pot boiling by raising the subject again and again. Meanwhile, the press badgered Ford unmercifully, asking him in press conference after press conference to either substantiate or withdraw his indefensible assertion about Poland. Ford, however, was slow to give in; finally he admitted that "I did not express myself clearly"—and then tried futilely to restate his point without denaturing it.

It is curious how many people share Gerald Ford's instinct to hang in there even though it is plain they have erred. Perhaps in this respect, as in so many others, he was Everyman. But no competent arguer would dream of trying to defend an indefensible point for an instant. Bear in mind that, as we noted at the outset, the competent arguer won't adopt a position in the first place unless he is absolutely sure it is defensible. Any error in his argumentation, therefore, is quite likely to be minor and capable of being abandoned without doing fatal damage to his basic contention. If, however, the error is indeed of dimensions that unavoidably spell the wreckage of his entire case, he will ordinarily abandon the latter *in toto* rather than plunge blindly on down the slope to sure defeat by his adversary.

A major example of this occurred in the lawsuit, already mentioned, that consumed most of three of the seven and a half years that I spent in the litigation department of Wall Street's biggest law firm. It will for this purpose be necessary to describe the key contention in that case in somewhat more detail.

Tabacalera, the Spanish-owned tobacco monopoly in the Philippines, had borrowed $2,800,000 from National City Bank before Pearl Harbor, then "repaid" it to the Japanese liquidator of NCB's Manila branch in Japanese occupation currency it had acquired by selling tobacco to Japanese troops. After the war Tabacalera and NCB agreed that this "repayment" was ineffective and, in return for fresh credits from the bank, Tabacalera began to repay the prewar debt in monthly installments. It had repaid $2,200,000 when the Philippine Supreme Court unexpectedly ruled, in an unrelated case, that repayment in Japanese occupation currency was a valid discharge of a prewar dollar debt.

Tabacalera of course now bitterly regretted its postwar agreement with NCB, and—alleging that the agreement was invalid because Tabacalera had had no independent legal advice on the validity of its wartime payments to the Japanese—sued NCB for the $2,200,000 already paid over to it after the war. NCB counterclaimed for the remaining $600,000, and the case came on in Supreme Court, New York County.

As noted in our earlier discussion of that case, the allegation that Tabacalera had had no independent legal advice was absolutely central to the undue-influence theory on which Tabacalera's own brand-new set of Wall Street lawyers was trying to overturn its postwar agreement with NCB. Our discovery in Tabacalera's files, therefore, of a 1943 communication from Tabacalera's Barcelona headquarters to its Manila representative, flatly asserting, with regard to the NCB loan, that "Lawyers . . . advise not to liquidate until end of war" was absolutely fatal. It led, in short order, to a settlement, in which Tabacalera paid $500,000 of the bank's $600,000 counterclaim. There was literally nothing else for Tabacalera to do.

If withdrawal is necessary, *how* ought one to withdraw? As I said earlier, there is nothing wrong with being inconspicuous about it if that is possible. There is no reason why the person withdrawing a contention need make a federal case out of it all by himself, and thereby advertise his error—unless, of course, it is some minor concession from which he hopes to earn points with a target audience for his scrupulousness and open-hearted candor in acknowledging it.

Even when a strategic retreat cannot be effectively concealed or minimized, however, it generally need not be unduly prolonged. Get it over with quickly and go on to something else—the more aggressive and effective the better.

For further instruction in this matter of withdrawal we shall turn once again to that master of argumentation, Sir Winston Churchill. The British House of Commons enforces an elaborate code of personal courtesy on its members, and when one of them transgresses it by calling, perhaps, some offensive statement "a lie," he will be sternly ordered by the Speaker to withdraw the offending remark, on pain of banishment from the House until he does so.

Once the House's lone Communist M.P., fiery Willie Gallacher from Glasgow, found himself under this painful necessity and was being stubborn about it. The Speaker rejected various alternative formulations of the offending expression. Churchill thereupon intervened in a friendly fashion and said, "If I may presume, as one who has often found himself in the same position, to offer some advice to the honorable member, the best way to withdraw is to withdraw."

And so it is—usually. Churchill himself, however, on one occasion made parliamentary history by persuading the Speaker to let him substitute, for the angry words "a lie," the exquisite formulation "a terminological inexactitude." (Note, as in the previously discussed case of Herr Hitler's impugned veracity, Churchill's sly use of Latin polysyllables to achieve a stressed effect by understatement.)

One final word. While mistakes ought to be admitted as promptly and economically as possible, care ought to be taken to fill the resulting hole in the line of argumentation. A faulty analogy should be replaced by a valid one, an erroneous quotation by an accurate one, etc. Mistakes properly handled usually do little harm, and in pure theory ought to do none *if* the gap in the argumentation is promptly filled.

WHEN YOUR OPPONENT MAKES A MISTAKE

Our discussion of how to deal with one's own errors makes it plain what we must hope for when an adversary blunders: i.e., that he will defend his mistake rather than admit it. An unadmitted mistake is like a wounded man on the battlefield: It requires constant attention, and is in imminent peril of being lost in any case. A competent arguer will exploit any such situation to the hilt, to his adversary's inevitable (and deserved) discomfiture. Unfortunately for competent arguers, their adversaries are usually competent too, so the opportunity to bully-rag such an unadmitted error is rare.

XI

VARIOUS KINDS OF ARGUMENTS

Thus far we have been dealing with basic matters applicable to all arguments: defining the issue, marshaling the arguments, putting a point across effectively. Now we shall turn to considerations applicable only to *specific kinds* of arguments.

Obviously, not all considerations are equally applicable to all kinds of arguments. If you must argue with your spouse, it is both appropriate and prudent to consider, and if possible to influence, where and when the argument will occur: in bed, over the breakfast table, or after dinner. If your argument is with the government, on the other hand, you will ordinarily have precious little choice in the matter: The argument will be held at a place and time of the government's choosing, and it assuredly won't be in bed.

Again, it is sometimes possible to choose the actual format of the argument, and this choice will naturally depend on which format seems likeliest to produce the result we want. Suppose a corporate vice-president wants to persuade his president to adopt some particular policy. Should he try to push for it over a round of golf? Or should he bring it up at a staff conference, where others will be present and can endorse (or oppose) the idea? Or should he stage it as an informal debate between friends and foes of the policy, perhaps at a meeting of the board of directors?

The above examples have already illustrated the four basic types of arguments:

1. *The informal personal argument.* This can arise with anyone we encounter in our daily lives: spouse, relatives, coworkers, friends

and acquaintances, schoolmates or teachers, and members of the general public such as cabdrivers, waiters, and store clerks.

2. *The argument with an institution*—typically government, although this category also includes arguments with business corporations, hospitals, and other non-governmental bureaucracies.

3. *The informal organized argument.* This covers all of those types of situations in which it is recognized that there are two or more sides to the matter up for discussion, and informal rules are devised to insure that all get a more or less equal airing.

4. *The formal organized argument.* This category includes all arguments that are conducted according to rigid and specific rules: lawsuits, formal debates of the intercollegiate type, even the deliberations of the U. S. Senate and House of Representatives. However, since congressional rules are of interest chiefly to congressmen, and legal procedures are a subject so vast that it is properly left to professional experts (i.e., lawyers), we will concern ourselves under this heading largely with college-type debates and their parallels.

What, then, are the considerations separately applicable to these four types of arguments?

THE INFORMAL PERSONAL ARGUMENT

The vast majority of all the arguments in the world are of this type, and the category suffers from their highly amorphous characteristics. A personal argument can blow up in an instant over nothing or next to nothing—and vanish a moment later, never to recur. It may take the form of coolly correct argumentation of a sort that would sound familiar at Oxford—or may be conducted exclusively at the level of a Dodger fan's yells at the opposing pitcher. In an effort to avoid getting bogged down in a wilderness of so-called "arguments" that are little more than exchanges of catcalls and vituperation, we will confine ourselves to personal arguments that involve at least some element of disagreement over a specific arguable issue.

The first thing the competent arguer in a personal argument of any kind will do is seek to isolate and identify the real issue—i.e., disentangle it from any merely emotional, visceral, or otherwise irrelevant draperies that may be hanging from it. These may include such familiar plaints as a wife's resentment of her sister-in-law, an employee's dislike of his job, or what have you. As we saw at the very outset of this book, personal arguments often mask resentments that it would be impolitic or downright dangerous to express directly. So the hidden animus is "displaced," as psychologists say, onto some other and safer object—and presto, an argument grows where none existed before.

C. S. Lewis included in his wonderful *Screwtape Letters* a superb description of how a long-smoldering resentment at one (deep) level can be fueled and tended until it breaks out at another and far more superficial one. Screwtape, the senior devil, is advising his nephew Wormwood, who has been apprenticed to him, on how to exacerbate the tensions between a mother and son who live together:

> Your patient must demand that all his own utterances are to be taken at their face value and judged simply on the actual words, while at the same time judging all his mother's utterances with the fullest and most oversensitive interpretation of the tone and the context and the suspected intention. She must be encouraged to do the same to him. Hence, from every quarrel they can both go away convinced, or very nearly convinced, that they are quite innocent. You know the kind of thing: "I simply ask her what time dinner will be and she flies into a temper."

We have all seen, over and over again in our own lives, examples of this sort of thing. As I suggested much earlier on, it may even have its virtues—focusing aggressions or resentments on irrelevant objects is often far safer than focusing them on their true targets.

But it is obviously pointless for a serious arguer to try to persuade, by logical argumentation on some issue, a person whose real (though unstated) purpose in pushing the point is to ventilate his hatred of (say) his father. So, as far as pursuit of the argument is concerned, all such emotional impediments should be spotted as soon as possible, brought to the surface, and formally expunged as legitimate factors for consideration.

Generally speaking, the more forthrightly this is done the better: "I know you won't let your dislike for your brother-in-law influence what you do for your sister's son." Most people appealed to in this way are fair-minded enough to correct, and even overcorrect, for their own emotional biases once these are pointed out to them.

Once the authentic issue in a personal argument has been isolated and identified, the argument itself is not far different in structure from any other: One marshals the evidence, makes one's points as effectively as possible, etc. Before a personal argument actually gets under way, however, there are often opportunities to shape it toward a favorable result.

Consider for example the matter of where it shall take place. As we saw earlier (p. 133), a spouse can frequently choose where an argument shall occur. Similarly, when a dispute looms between business colleagues it can often be defused—or won—by changing its locale. If it breaks out on the phone, "Let's discuss it over lunch" gives both sides a chance to cool down, and transfers the argument to a traditionally friendly arena. If you have a choice in the matter, holding the argument in your office often gives you a heavy psychological advantage. Conversely, there is usually something a little intimidating or otherwise unsatisfactory about arguing with a cabdriver in his cab, or with a teacher in the schoolroom, or with a clerk in his store. If possible, argue with such people on neutral ground— or better yet on your own.

What is true of picking the place for an argument is often equally true of picking its time. Merely postponing it is frequently a good idea if possible—to cool the protagonists, enable them to plan their arguments, and afford time to recruit allies. (Conversely, of course, an arguer already well-prepared in these respects may want to push the argument along as fast as possible, to exploit his advantage.)

For the rest, the general rules of argumentation are the ones that apply to personal arguments. In "one-on-one" situations (e.g., husband vs. wife) the adversaries may know each other's wiles so well that even local successes are rare and true "victory" almost impossible. But the traditional rules nevertheless apply, and expertise in this type of argument is readily transferable to more consciously structured types.

ARGUING WITH AN INSTITUTION

There is, however, one type of argument the rules and strategy of which are *sui generis,* and it will be well to deal with it here before resuming the discussion of more orthodox types. I refer to arguing with an institution.

Of course, a purely orthodox argument with an institution is quite conceivable—in fact, they occur every day in the form of individuals' lawsuits against business corporations, or communications between two corporations, whether the communication takes the form of a lawsuit or not. (It is a curious fact that corporations take each other more seriously than they take individual human beings, rather like two dogs on a crowded street.)

In all such cases the general rules of argumentation, outlined in earlier chapters, apply. And it is only fair to acknowledge, in addition, that some business corporations manage to feign (it is rarely more than that, outside the Legal Department) a personal interest in individuals, and to do business with them in a meretriciously "personalized" way. As anybody knows, however, who has ever, for no matter how good a reason, refused to pay a bill to some large business enterprise that monitors such matters by computer, traditional forms of rational argumentation with its mechanized Credit Department are quite out of the question.

A prime illustration of the genre is the battle I am currently having with Visa, the credit-card people. I have not yet gotten around to applying to Visa the tried-and-true rules set forth later in this chapter —but I will, I will. Meanwhile, Visa is providing this book with a superb example of institutional bureaucracy at its worst.

For some reason known only to itself (I suspect it is in order to euchre your account into overdue status and charge you interest on it), Visa is not content to advise you monthly what you owe it.* That figure (called the "new balance") is only the third of four separate figures on your statement. First you are advised of your "total credit line"; then of your "available credit"; then of your "new bal-

* My quarrel with Visa, and its procedures as described above, antedate the 1980 tightening in credit card procedures as an anti-inflation measure.

ance"; and finally of your "total minimum payment"—which sounds like the amount due but is in fact a smaller sum, arrived at I know not how. This, it transpires, is what Visa really wants you to pay—the unpaid remainder of your debt being carried forward at your (inferred) request, with interest being charged on it.

Two or three years ago, tiring of the complexities of Visa's self-serving bookkeeping, I notified Visa that I wanted to terminate my account with it. In accordance with its telephonic instructions, I cut the card into irregular pieces and mailed the pieces to Visa.

Unfortunately I had, a month or two previously, inquired about a $59.65 charge to my account, attributed merely to "STEM/SHOP." I couldn't recall the charge, or "STEM/SHOP," or imagine for the life of me what the charge might have been. (A pipe? I don't smoke.) I so advised Visa. Visa, taking the position—apparently necessary from the standpoint of its rigid procedures—that I was challenging the charge (which was not true—I was merely asking what it was *for*), moved the $59.65 item into a "suspense file" while it went on what became a six-month hunt for the original charge voucher. When ultimately located, this turned out to be for a pair of shoes bought at Lloyd & Haig (the decoded identity of "STEM/SHOP"). I promptly remembered the transaction and paid the bill.

End of story? I wish it were! Visa, apparently unable to leave the $59.65 charge in its suspense file until the matter was resolved, had taken it upon itself after some months to *credit* my account with that amount, and now tells me I cashed a Visa check for that figure. I have no recollection of having done so, but it certainly is possible that I did; I have simply asked Visa to send me a photostat of the cashed check, whereupon I will promptly reimburse them.

There the matter stands—except for Visa's computer and its human servitors. Visa's computer understands only that I owe Visa $59.65, and interest has been charged on this sum for nearly a year. Recently, therefore, I began getting mysterious monthly bills showing $15.00 (don't ask me why $15.00) as my "new balance" and $5.00 as my "total minimum payment." A telephone call to Visa elicited portions of the above story, plus a request that I state my position in writing—which I did.

Subsequently I have received from Visa several further monthly bills for varying amounts, a sharp notice that my credit is being suspended, and five phone calls from separate Visa representatives, all of them unaware of my letter or phone calls or of each other. (The first representative advised me to ignore all bills and written threats generated by the computer, since my letter is presumably being investigated and acted upon.) It is also possible, though fortunately unlikely, that Visa's computer will lose its patience and order my credit rating impaired before human hands can turn it off. In that case, Visa will have a nice fat little lawsuit for credit defamation on its hands.

Meanwhile, the whole episode is thoroughly reflective of the sort of argument almost everybody has, sooner or later, with the machines that conduct most corporate transactions with the public these days. The situation is usually even worse if a person happens to be arguing with some branch of government rather than a private corporation, for then there will be added to the mechanical rigidity of corporate business practices the indifference, ineptitude, and sheer insolence that often characterize the responses of government. (As Churchill once prophetically remarked of civil servants, they tend to become "no longer servants, and no longer civil.")

What to do? The formula for winning an argument with an institution is simple, and involves two steps:

1. As in the case of the mule whose owner firmly believed in kindness but was seen beating the stubborn animal on the head with a two-by-four, you must first get the institution's attention.

2. Then, on strict pleasure-pain principles, you must persuade the institution that it will be less painful to do whatever it is you want it to do than to go on *not* doing it.

Getting the attention of a large and rigidly bureaucratic institution, of course, is usually no easy matter; in fact, inattention is one of the great institutional defenses. Look at Visa: It has designed a series of automatic procedures which are failing to do the job, either because they were badly designed or (more likely) because they are being applied to a wider range of situations than they were designed to cover. They serve, however, even while they malfunction, to keep up a drumfire of petty harassments against people from whom Visa wants something (usually money), and eight or nine times out of ten they "work," in a crude sort of way. Thus in my case, Visa's experience undoubtedly tells it (or would if a human intelligence were focused on the matter) that the chances are I will crumple sooner or later under the steady drumfire of phone calls and bills for various "new balances" and "total minimum payments." And anyway, even if I don't crumple, the whole fuss over my alleged account will ultimately generate so much paperwork at Visa that it will levitate straight out of the computer and the lower levels of human harassment onto the desk of some person with enough intelligence to understand the problem and enough authority to resolve it.

The objective I have called "getting their attention" is simply the speeding up of this natural process.

How to speed up the process? There is, after all, no reason why I should spend my declining years exchanging letters and phone calls on this pitiful little matter, waiting for the paperwork to reach whatever passes for critical mass over at Visa. The winning technique is to overleap the whole computer process and *involve some competent authority right away* in the resolution of the problem.

In practice this means, in the case of a corporation, exciting the interest of a top executive or a house lawyer. In the case of government, the prevailing climate of indifference renders this less effective, but happily there is a third and very choice target: some politician—usually a congressman—on whose favor the bureaucracy in question depends.

Let's take those means of getting attention one at a time. In my own small way, as publisher of *National Review*, I rank as a "top executive," and there is just no denying that a subscriber's letter of complaint, directed to me, gets special attention. Fortunately, our circulation department under the imperturbable John Syze is currently doing its job so efficiently that few complaints arise. Moreover, the department's skill and speed in handling those that do arise are so impressive that there is seldom occasion for anybody (save cranks actually *looking* for trouble) to write to me over its head. Every so often, however, a complaint letter does reach my desk. Naturally, I pass it along to Syze for his attention—and inevitably, whatever maltreatment the subscriber has (or has not) received in the past, that letter *does* get Syze's personal attention.

In the case of larger businesses, of course, catching the eye or ear of a top executive isn't so easy. His secretary may have standing orders to refer all complaint letters of a certain sort to Mr. X; but you can be sure Mr. X knows that letters to the boss, received for action from the boss' personal secretary, are not lightly to be disregarded.

For added clout the executive's attention may at times (if you have some suitable means) be engaged indirectly but publicly. For example, I have no doubt that when this book is published it will generate inquiries from (inter alia) the top echelons of Visa to working stiffs down the line, concerning the outcome of my current flap with them. No executive could possibly enjoy a public description of his bureaucracy's performance as uncomplimentary as the one I have given of Visa's, and some will care enough to try to intervene. With luck it will all have been straightened out by then; but if it hasn't, I think I can promise you that within two months after this book hits the stores, it will be.

A useful variant of the top-executive gambit, when it comes to focusing competent human attention on a problem with an institution, is to involve its lawyers. Behind all computers, at the right hand of every executive, monitoring the performance of all lesser employees, every sizable institution has its lawyers. In a small business like *National Review* it may be an outside attorney or firm (though, as a lawyer myself, I serve as house counsel to some undefined degree), but practically every large business has full-time attorneys on its own staff. In many cases—and spectacularly in cases involving credit, like Visa—these attorneys may be assigned directly to the handling of any problems that the computers and the telephonic pesterers don't seem to be coping with effectively. To precipitate a problem into the lap of such a house lawyer is to have it well on its way to a solution.

Nika Hazelton, who writes for *National Review* on cooking and related delightful matters, recently told her readers in an aside that one sure-fire way of breaking through bureaucratic defenses and forcing competent attention to a problem is to ask (say) a telephonic pesterer sharply, "Are you authorized by your company to talk about a matter that might lead to litigation?" Since the pesterer invariably isn't, this implied threat of legal action often results in prompt referral of the whole matter to house counsel, with whom it can then be discussed and settled intelligently.

More drastic but even surer ways of reaching the institution's attorneys include the explicit written threat (or announcement) of legal action, or—better yet, if you have a friend who is a lawyer—a letter on an attorney's letterhead. Once again, as in the case of dogs and corporations, nothing grabs the attention of a lawyer like the arrival on the scene of another lawyer. That is because he senses (correctly) that the argument may be about to escalate, and that the time has therefore come to start taking it seriously.

Symmetry would dictate that, before going on to a discussion of the second principle to be remembered in arguing with institutions (i.e., persuading it, on pure pleasure-pain principles, to do what needs doing), I should apply the first principle—getting its attention —to that most recalcitrant of all institutions: government. But getting government's attention and moving it to action are often achieved by the same dramatic means, which it will be simpler to discuss and illustrate just once, a bit later. Let us consider now, therefore, how to obtain some desired action from a non-governmental institution, once its attention has been won.

In what follows, I assume that the action desired is some proper one—i.e., something to which the person seeking the action is in fact legitimately entitled. If however there are any doubts on this score, they must be faced and eliminated as in any other argument: by adducing relevant principles, marshaling the factual evidence, etc. Obviously, a corporation or other institution is at least as unlikely as any other adversary or target audience to take some action it considers not only undesirable but unjustified.

But merely showing an institution that it *ought* to take some specific action in a particular matter may not always be the same thing as actually persuading it to *do* so. In the case of a reasonably efficient and fair-minded business corporation, getting its attention may indeed be 90 percent of the battle: It will, in its own interest, want to do the right thing once the problem has been called forcibly to its attention and it has been convinced that a given action is indeed the right one to take. But a really large and arthritic corporate bureaucracy may be almost as inert as a government agency. Something more than justice must be on our side. What can it be?

As usual in human affairs self-interest is the queen of motives here, and if such higher considerations related to self-interest as good will are too gossamer to rouse a sluggish corporate bureaucrat, it is often possible to stir him to action by application of a suitable specific discomfort. When the discomfort applied becomes greater than the discomfort involved in taking the desired action—or, in other words, when on straight pleasure-pain principles it costs him more to refuse than to comply—he will comply.

What motivating discomfort can the average person apply directly to a torpid corporate bureaucrat? I suggest that it is usually possible to worry him that *his own personal name* may be dragged into the matter, in some public or semi-public way. Mr. John Jones, time-serving corporate hack, may be totally indifferent to a warning that hereafter you will think less of General Motors, yet he will leap like Nijinsky at the suggestion that his own name, linked to a charge of incompetence or dereliction (or both), may even now be in a letter lying on the desk of GM's president. A *fortiori* if you can plausibly threaten to have an account of his sins of omission or commission published in the newspapers.

There, I admit, is where it helps to have a newspaper column of one's own, as I do. Some years ago our bookkeeper at *National Review* discovered that I had, three months before, been summarily removed from *National Review's* Blue Cross medical plan (of which I had been a contented member for fifteen years) and included in the plan of the American Federation of Television and Radio Artists, a union to which I didn't even belong. Apparently I had simply been inhaled by AFTRA, the way a whale inhales a minnow, because I occasionally appear on TV. What's more, Blue Cross had obeyed AFTRA's sovereign instruction in the matter of medical plans, not only without consulting me but without even informing me!

Almost shaking with rage—I had never felt more manhandled in my life—I phoned Blue Cross's office and was finally referred to some nail-polishing young lady who told me Blue Cross could do nothing—I would have to "straighten the matter out with AFTRA" (to which I had never even spoken!). When I had absorbed this advice, I obtained from her the name of her superior officer (always useful, and difficult to withhold), and told her that, on the contrary, I fully expected to be out of AFTRA's plan and back in *National Review*'s by the close of business that very day, without ever speaking to AFTRA at all. A bold prediction, but I estimated that my head of steam, plus the threat of my column, made it a realistic one.

And so it came to pass. When the smoke blew away toward the sunset I was holding in my hand the written and signed assurance of a Blue Cross official who didn't want his name in the papers that I was indeed out of the AFTRA plan and back in *National Review*'s, effective retroactively for the whole three-month period involved.

Bill Buckley, whose column is far more widely syndicated than my own, has repeatedly used it, or (more broadly) the celebrity deriving from it and his other activities, to get action in situations not to his liking. (Of course, neither of us would employ our column in a purely personal argument—it must, like my quarrel with AFTRA, be one in which the columnist is in effect an ombudsman for a larger class of people subject to victimization in the same way.) Some years ago, on an Eastern Airlines plane bound for Florida, Buckley was deprived of wine with his lunch because the flight was not at least three hours' long. Thereafter, flying to Miami, he would send postcards to the president of Eastern describing the pleasures of the wine aboard National Airlines. This finally not only resulted in changing Eastern's policy in regard to wine on short flights, but netted him a large basket of select bottles and the compliments of the airline.

But the average citizen can stir, or at least plausibly threaten to stir, a sizable ruckus even if he doesn't happen to have regular personal access to the media. Many newspapers have an "Action Line" —a column to which citizens can address their complaints against private or public institutions. The newspaper will then investigate the complaint and report the result in print—a splendid example of compelling action through the threat of publicity. Where no such service exists, a letter to your local newspaper or television station (with a copy to the offending institution) can often get results, even if the newspaper or station has no "Action Line" and does nothing whatever.

Everything thus far said about winning an argument with a corporation applies to arguments with government—only more so. Government is not only the largest but the most sluggish of all institutions, the most impervious to efforts to get its attention, the most resistant to small discomforts, the least moved by the justice of a petitioner's cause. This is partly owing to its sheer size and partly to the extremely poor quality of many of the employees in its lower echelons. In an informal but real way, government is in many cases our employer of last resort—the institution that will hire people who are too incompetent or just plain too lazy to get work elsewhere. The citizens who then have to deal with these myrmidons are the ones who must suffer.

How can a mere human being hope to win an argument with such a monster? Writing it in a letter will ordinarily result only in a routine reply (months later) instructing you to fill out the enclosed forms, in triplicate, and send them to some office for action that never occurs. Going to a government office in person invariably involves long waits in uncomfortable places—followed by the aforesaid forms and instructions. Phoning will only elicit the information that nothing can be done over the phone.

Slowly you will realize that government's necessity, real or supposed, to make written records of everything is at the heart of its brilliant Fabian tactics. The demand for more and more paperwork will ultimately overwhelm any effort, no matter how determined or sustained, to achieve any concrete result whatever.

(I am speaking here, of course, of a result that a citizen wants *from government*. Results that government wants *from a citizen*— e.g., tax payments—are handled efficiently, even peremptorily, and usually by a category and quality of government employee very different from that assigned to wait on the citizenry.)

This torpor of government, where responses to citizens are concerned, is so near-total that it is already spawning entire new categories of experts who specialize in calling the just claims of helpless citizens to the government's attention and then following through until the desired action is obtained.

The most famous such specialists are the ombudsmen—those publicly paid functionaries, originating in the Scandinavian countries (where socialist bureaucracies rule so much of people's lives), whose assignment is to hear and help citizens who are entitled to some sort of government action. The word, and to some degree the function, has caught on in this country, even in the case of certain non-governmental institutions (cf. William Seib, the Washington *Post*'s resident ombudsman, to whom complaints against that newspaper's coverage of a story may be submitted). But the American society was already devising its own answer to the problem long before the concept of the ombudsman ever reached our shores.

Every senator and representative maintains at least one office (and often several, strategically located around his district or state) to handle what is called "case work." This is the daily grist of requests and complaints from constituents, usually but not always involving government, and members of Congress are generally only too happy to "be of service" to voters by forwarding any reasonable request to the appropriate bureaucrat, along with a covering letter asking for prompt action. They will also usually help a bewildered citizen obtain and fill out necessary forms, and if necessary assist in deciding (it may not always be clear) what his problem is.

Congressional staff budgets include specific allocations for employees to handle such case work: welfare problems, passport and immigration requests, matters affecting veterans or current members of the armed forces, etc., etc. These employees can be of very considerable help to an otherwise helpless citizen, because in the vast federal bureaucracy itself certain specially efficient employees in every major department, agency, and office are assigned solely to handle inquiries and requests emanating from Capitol Hill. This is not merely a matter of inter-branch courtesy: The executive departments are dependent for their own funds on the good will of Congress, and it behooves them to keep on good terms with the hand that feeds them.

A request in (say) an immigration matter, received by the Immigration Service through the mails from some faceless individual in Trenton, New Jersey, simply isn't in the same league with an identical request forwarded through the office of a senator or congressman from New Jersey. They don't even reach the same desk: The former will get whatever routine treatment the Immigration Service affords;

the latter will be received and processed by the Service's "legislative liaison" facilities.

It is not hard to envision developing here, among the congressional staff employees who handle case work, a wholly new profession: a class of special intervenors, trained to represent citizens in their dealings with the bureaucracy, just as "barristers" developed in England in the Middle Ages out of the group of spokesmen who specialized in representing ordinary folk before the bar of the King's courts. Today's new class is not likely to get that far, however, because lawyers have already preempted the ground. Any really important action that a citizen wants government to take—granting a patent, for example, or an export license—already requires a lawyer. And, of course, at still higher levels, the relations between the bureaucracy and the rest of society (corporate as well as individual) are simply one vast happy hunting ground for lawyers, on both sides.

Still, for many lesser purposes a citizen with a complaint against government—federal, state, or local—will do well to invoke the aid of his senator or representative or some other attentive politician. The practice is now so common that here and there it is itself getting somewhat bureaucratized and routinized. (One must always be on the lookout for the politician whose services are available for a fee— i.e., a bribe.) But by and large the political route to action is an effective one.

If you are reluctant to incur an obligation to such a politician (not that I encourage you to feel any—helping constituents is partly what he's paid for), the political route can often still be used to bestir a government bureaucracy to action. Many years ago—nearly thirty, in fact—the Veterans Administration owed me $210: part, I believe, of whatever reimbursement it was then making to veterans in connection with excessive premiums charged and paid on their GI life insurance. The debt was indisputable; unfortunately I had moved from Boston to New York not long before, when I graduated from Harvard Law School and went to work for a Wall Street law firm, and the VA's records on my case were somewhere in limbo between New York and Boston. Nothing could be done; or at any rate nothing *was* done—and in those days $210 was not only worth a lot more than it is today, but I was a lot younger and poorer.

A phone call to the VA office in New York informed me that my only hope was to appear there in person and state my case. On my lunch hour, therefore, I made my way from Wall Street up to 260 Broadway. There, in the VA office, I finally found the line I was supposed to join. It not only stretched for the better part of a city block, filled with hapless wretches each of whose problems would obviously take an afternoon to solve if they could be solved at all, but ended at a single counter where numbered tickets were dispensed. The lucky holder of such a ticket was entitled to go to an area with benches, and to sit on one until his number was called. Presumably at that point somebody would hear him out, give him forms to fill out in triplicate (maybe even help him fill them out), and tell him he would be informed in due course—the twenty-first century?—of whatever action had been taken on his request.

Meanwhile my lunch hour was nearly over, and I hadn't even joined the line!

Returning to my office, I did a bit of research and then called in a secretary and dictated several letters, all marked "Personal" and "Urgent" and all Registered with Return Receipt Requested. The first was addressed, by name, to General Omar Bradley, then director of the Veterans Administration. It began by saying I wanted to call to his attention an error made by Mr. So-and-so (I forget the name), head of the New York office of the Veterans Administration at 260 Broadway. I then outlined my right to the $210, and my failure to receive same, and closed by expressing the hope that General Bradley would take whatever steps were necessary to bring order out of the chaos in his New York office.

The second letter was addressed to Hon. Irving Ives, then Senator from New York. I reminded Senator Ives (who would surely have needed reminding) that we had met briefly on the occasion of his visit to a state Young Republican convention the year before. I then duplicated the basic thrust of my letter to General Bradley.

The third letter was addressed to my own Congressman, Hon. Frederic R. Coudert, Jr. I had met Coudert a few times, but more to the point on this occasion was the fact, which I stressed, that I was at this time a Republican election district captain in the congressman's district. The rest of the letter followed the lines of those to Bradley and Ives.

I believe I may also have sent copies of the Bradley letter to the chairmen of the Veterans' Affairs Committees of the House and Senate, asking them to investigate the deplorable state of affairs at 260 Broadway and demanding my $210, but if so it was overkill and I knew it.

I then sent carbon copies (these were the days before Xerox) of all these letters to Mr. So-and-so at 260 Broadway—Personal, Urgent, Registered, Return Receipt Requested—and sat back to await results.

For two weeks, nothing. I believe I did get a polite routine acknowledgment from Coudert's office, and later another from Ives, indicating that some case worker had forwarded my complaint to the VA's legislative liaison office for action; but I knew very little in those days about case work, let alone legislative liaison offices, and it was really Mr. So-and-so on whom I was counting.

He did not disappoint me. Two weeks after my letters went out, a check for $210 suddenly arrived from 260 Broadway—and in a matter of days another, also for $210, from the VA office in Washington! (I returned the latter, of course, with a dry note.) Verily, as the elder Oliver Wendell Holmes remarked, "It's the squeaky wheel that gets the oil."

To sum up, then, on the subject of arguing with institutions, whether private or governmental: It will seldom be enough for you to have justice on your side. You must first get the beast's attention, and then you must stir it to the desired action on pure pleasure-pain principles. In capturing the attention of a non-governmental institution, it will normally be helpful to go directly to top executives—or to the institution's lawyers, if these can be located and approached. Once its attention has been obtained, a non-governmental institution may well be decent and energetic enough to do the right thing. If it isn't, the threat of internal publicity (calling the bureaucrat's own name to the critical attention of his superiors) or external publicity (focusing public attention on the entire institution in a negative way) will often produce results.

With government, the sovereign instruments for winning attention *and* favorable action are the politicians on whom the bureaucrats in question must rely. And the heavier the reliance, the better. If, let us say, it is the Agriculture Department that must be moved, Senator D'Amato will do in a pinch; but a member of the House or Senate Agriculture Committee is obviously preferable, and the chairman of either is practically a living Open Sesame. (A less obvious ally, but in some ways an even more influential one, is some member of that subcommittee of the Senate Finance Committee or House Ways and Means Committee that passes on the budget requests of the agency in question. Just watch the bureaucrats jump when *he* writes or phones!)

Of course, in addition to everything else one must be in the right in one's arguments with government. Government normally won't crumple before unmerited claims—nor should it. But nowhere else will merely "having the better side of the argument" do you so little good. One must not only be right, but knowledgeable and aggressive, to prevail against a governmental institution.

ORGANIZED ARGUMENTS

Most arguments arise on an *ad hoc* basis, developing more or less unexpectedly out of some preexisting situation. They are then fought out informally, or if they are serious enough, transferred to a court and fought out very formally indeed.

In between the informal argument and the court case, however, there is another type of argument with which we are all familiar: the organized argument. This may take the form of a formal or informal debate, or it may be called a panel, a symposium, a round table, or something else not quite so unnervingly aggressive as "a debate." In any case, the usual purpose of organizing this kind of argument is to generate a certain amount of enlightenment—for the participants, the audience, or both—so the stress is on cordiality. There may even be a genuine desire to reach a measure of agreement, by persuasion or compromise, though the organizers and the audiences of even the most sweetly inoffensive "symposium" are often secretly grateful for an occasional sharp clash of opinions, just to perk things up.

In any event, the organizer of such an affair has various decisions to make at the very outset. Shall it be billed as a "debate" or something less intimidating? Ordinarily a "debate" is an argument in which two or more different points of view (preferably not too many) are put forward without much expectation that they will converge toward agreement as the discussion goes on: Televised arguments between candidates during an election campaign are in this category; so are arguments before the Oxford and Cambridge Unions, or other college forensic contests.

On the other hand, it may be that there are four, five, or even more viewpoints to be aired, or a subject to be discussed from several different but not necessarily clashing angles (e.g., political, economic, sociological, and theological); or perhaps there is a real hope that the protagonists, sharply divided at the start, will reach agreement or at least usefully define and perhaps narrow their differences by the time the discussion is over. Such an argument (which may be only partly an "argument" anyway) is best labeled a "panel" if it has not more than five or six participants and takes place before an audience, and a "round table," "symposium," or "conference" if a larger group, especially without an exterior audience, is involved.

Don't let the general atmosphere of cordiality dull your wits, however, if you happen to be recruited to take part in such an affair. A common desire for enlightenment is not necessarily inconsistent with an individual desire to stress a point, "stand out," or even carry the day. It is safest, at any rate, to assume that one or more of your fellow panelists or conferees has some such intention and to be ready to counter him to any necessary extent. Here, then, are a few things to bear in mind if and when you are asked to take part in one of these organized but relatively informal arguments—a "panel," or whatever.

INFORMAL ORGANIZED ARGUMENTS

As with any other argument, incomparably the most important datum about any panel, round table, symposium, or conference is its exact topic. Everything, therefore, that was said earlier on that subject applies here. A very broad or ill-defined topic ("Poverty," "Busing," "Tax Policy in the Years Ahead") may not matter much if no particular outcome is sought or expected, and too narrow a topic may actually inhibit the discussion unless somebody deliberately dis-regards the topic's stated limits. But ordinarily a panel, conference, etc. will benefit markedly from having a topic that is defined with reasonable precision.

In informal arguments of the kind we are now discussing, much necessarily also depends upon the competence of the chairman or other presiding officer. Its very informality means that it will be up to him to get the discussion rolling, keep it within bounds, make sure that everybody gets a chance to speak and that no one hogs the floor, and wrap up the discussion when it's gone on long enough. The chairman should be picked, therefore, with great care.

If you attend many conferences, you will soon note that the real masters of the genre almost never are among the first to speak. On a panel, it may be difficult to control one's place in the speaking sequence—most panel chairmen will just arbitrarily call on the other members in what might be called geographical order: from left to right, or vice versa. But in a conference or other larger group, partici-pants ordinarily speak whenever they are moved to do so, and the competent arguer will be in no hurry to chime in. Listen to the drift of the other speakers; follow the thread of the discussion. Identify the majority and minority views, spot the weaknesses in the argu-ments that are made, decide what you want to say and how best to say it—and then say it as well as you possibly can. It may even be possible to summarize and synthesize what earlier speakers have said, making your own contribution the capstone of the whole discussion —a capstone designed, naturally, to stress the points you want to stress. (Chief Justice Burger was recently accused, in *The Brethren*, of abusing the Chief Justice's privilege of assigning the Court's opin-ion, when he was with the majority. Burger would allegedly assign the opinion to himself so that he could stress or soften particular points.)

If the format permits repartee among the participants, all of the rhetorical devices discussed earlier can be used. And, whether they can or not, the basic principles of effective argumentation apply to panels, conferences, etc. precisely as they do to any other form of ar-gument. It may be necessary, however, just because the argument is so unstructured, to take more than ordinary care to make sure that you get the necessary time to state your points, answer attacks on them, and rebut or endorse the statements of other participants.

Ordinarily, the simpler the format of an informal organized argument, the better. In the traditional three- or four-person panel, each person is invited by the chairman to make a brief opening statement; then the discussion is "opened up" for an unstructured give-and-take among the panelists; and finally the audience is invited to ask them questions. (The other panelists are often allowed to comment, if they wish, on the answer a colleague has given.) A brief closing summary by each panelist may also be requested. This is a fair and thoroughly serviceable format, usable for almost any topic.

Provided the organizers of the panel have a clear notion of what they want to accomplish, however, and keep a tight rein on the proceedings, far more complex formats have been tried successfully. Not long ago I was part of a six-person panel discussion—two economists, two consumer advocates, and two "generalists" (one liberal and one conservative in each case)—that took place during a session of the annual convention of a large national trade association. The organizers planned to divide the session into three segments of 30, 60, and 45 minutes each, separated by fifteen-minute coffee breaks. During the first segment each panelist would be introduced and asked to speak for about four minutes. During the second, we would be questioned by a separate panel of three journalists from the trade press— one question per journalist per panelist, or eighteen in all. During the third segment there would be questions from the floor.

Frankly, I was not optimistic about the success of the format. It sounded overloaded, and as intricately choreographed as a ballet—a ballet, moreover, with no time for rehearsals! Yet the surprising fact is that the whole thing went very well—thanks largely to the organizers' insistence on sticking to their timetable and making sure that the program's participants understood it and stuck to it too. The audience was delighted, and several members of it later told me it had been one of the best panels they had ever watched.

If there are no closing summaries by the panelists, or in the case of larger groups where individual summaries would obviously be impractical, it will generally be helpful if the chairman makes a few concluding remarks thanking the participants, reviewing the main themes developed in the discussion, pinpointing any lady-or-tiger issues remaining unresolved, and pronouncing the whole affair worthwhile. The British are more attentive to this detail than many American chairmen, and I have found it a graceful coda to many evenings that might otherwise linger in memory as a little ragged.

FORMAL ORGANIZED ARGUMENTS

The formally structured debate has come down in the world, but it hasn't disappeared altogether and probably never will. Like boxing, it pits fairly equal antagonists against each other under strictly controlled conditions, and the outcome is largely determined by their respective skills. Watching a really good debate, therefore, affords much the same sort of satisfaction as watching an evenly matched sporting contest, save that the exertions are primarily intellectual, or at least rhetorical, rather than physical. A cogent point, a barbed remark, a witty retort, a crushing rejoinder, a fine peroration—each is appreciated by a debate audience as much as the crowd enjoys a tense volley in tennis or a pitching duel in baseball.

Precisely because formal debates are designed to be carefully balanced, with each side having a reasonable chance to win, there will usually be little opportunity to manipulate the topic to favor one side or the other. The national college debating fraternity, Pi Kappa Delta, which annually specifies one topic of national interest for debate, usually picks topics that give both sides plenty of ammunition, and phrases the question so as not to favor one side over the other.

Similarly, because of the formality of the rules, this sort of argument leaves little room for a competent arguer to maneuver himself into speaking second (say), or having the last word: The rules will determine, all too inexorably, who has the affirmative, who speaks first, who speaks second, who gets the last word, etc. On the other hand, being fair and reasonable rules intended to apply over a wide range of topics and situations, they generally distribute these little advantages pretty evenly between the two sides. The grossest injustices in such matters are usually committed by inexperienced organizers who are simply improvising and aren't even aware that they are being unjust.

The aforementioned evenhandedness of the typical debate topic, and the consequent higher relative emphasis on debating *technique* (style and tactics, or if you prefer, "tricks"), underlie one serious criticism of formal debating, especially as this art is still taught in some colleges today.

In order to train the apprentice debater to make the best possible use of his resources, both substantive and stylistic, two debaters, or two teams of debaters, are sometimes instructed to prepare to debate *either* side of a particular question. Then, only moments before the debate is to begin, they flip a coin and determine thereby who shall take which side. The gavel falls and the debate is on—sometimes so fast that the first speaker can hardly locate his relevant notes in time. A moment later he may be directing withering scorn at some policy proposal that, three minutes earlier, he was perfectly prepared to praise to the skies.

Theodore Roosevelt, for one, thought it was highly immoral to train boys in this way to argue, with equal facility, out of either side of their mouth. A man should argue, Roosevelt insisted, only for a cause in which he truly believes.

As it happens I agree with Roosevelt's basic dictum, but don't object to the particular training tactic he deplored. One of the most valuable qualities of a competent arguer is his ability to anticipate what his opponent is going to say, and there is no better way to cultivate that ability than by shouldering the burden of constructing those arguments oneself. I have never in my life since leaving college taken the side in a debate with which I personally disagreed, but I have made it a point to understand my opponents' arguments just as well as I possibly could—the better to combat them. And for that purpose there is simply nothing quite like "putting yourself in your opponent's shoes."

Should there be a "decision" at the close of a formal debate, and if so who should make it? In this democratic era it seems inevitable that most of the time any decision that is reached will be by a simple vote of the audience. When I was in college just before World War II, however, formal debates were quite frequently judged by a three-man panel of distinguished oldsters (often literally judges from nearby courts). They listened attentively to the arguments made, assessed the personal skills of the debaters, and reached their decision on a sort of point-score basis, handing it up to the chairman like the judges in a prize-fight—and often with as much indifference to the opinion of the crowd.

To a serious debater, that is surely a better way of evaluating a hard-fought argument than leaving the outcome up to a vote by an audience that may well be biased or inattentive or both. But in a world where majority opinion counts for so much, the ability to sway a crowd is in many situations more valuable than the ability to state a truly polished and persuasive case.

RADIO AND TELEVISION ARGUMENTS
(DEBATES, PANELS, ETC.)

Radio and television are so pervasive in our lives these days that any man or woman in the middle or higher level of business, or who becomes involved in politics or community affairs at any level from the PTA on up, is quite likely to receive an invitation to participate in some argument that is going to be broadcast—usually in the form of a "panel," less often a "debate." For some reason this strikes terror in many hearts that ought to be made of more durable stuff. Arguing on radio or TV is no different from arguing off of them—with certain exceptions, of which this section takes notice.

First, however, the main point: The general rules of argumentation, as laid down in preceding chapters, apply with equal or even greater force to arguments on radio and TV. Since the *purpose* of a broadcast argument is almost always to persuade the audience "out there," the arguer on radio or TV must never forget that the audience *is* out there. Occasionally I have seen somebody forget that, almost always with unfortunate results.

My colleague Bill Buckley, for example, has in various presidential election years formed a twosome with John Kenneth Galbraith to get up early during the Republican and Democratic conventions and offer on the "Today" show a little joint commentary on the preceding day's developments. Now, Buckley and Galbraith, though they disagree on just about everything in the realms of politics and economics, are close personal friends, at least partly because Buckley cannot resist any genuinely witty person, and Galbraith is one of the wittiest human beings alive. On the air, however, Galbraith's wit, however silkily it may be deployed, is always at the service of his razor-sharp brain and its leftist politics; whereas Bill, knowing that nothing much hangs on the outcome of these discussions, tends to surrender himself to the voluptuous pleasure of simply enjoying Galbraith's wisecracks. The result, more than once, has been that Buckley has settled for being little more than Galbraith's straight man— to the understandable distress of conservative viewers like myself. (I once finally spoke to Bill about this, and was relieved to note that the next morning's discussion was far more even-handed.)

In the case of "The Advocates," where the objective was to persuade the largest possible number of viewers to send in their postcard votes in my favor, I never permitted myself to forget, even for a moment, the hundreds of thousands or millions of people who were watching on television the little arena, containing three desks and a "witness stand," in which our arguments took place. And it was particularly tempting to forget them, because there was also always a "live audience" of anywhere from 75 to 250, recruited by the producing station locally to provide spontaneous applause and other reactions.

This live audience, especially in the case of shows produced by WGBH-TV in Boston, was politically speaking almost always well to the left of the general sentiments of the national audience watching the show on TV. Many stations of the Public Broadcasting System are affiliated with universities or other educational institutions, and thus are located in college towns. Most of the rest, as one would expect of an "educational" network, attract viewers of a rather intellectual stripe. The national viewing audience for PBS, therefore, undoubtedly is more liberal in its political preferences than those watching (say) Johnny Carson or a pro football game.* But even the national audience was well to the right of the sentiments typically on

* Which of course is why I am especially proud that, arguing the conservative side of the question on fifty-eight "Advocates" programs, I won the vote of the national TV audience thirty-three times.

display among our live audience when the show was produced in Boston. There I could always count on enthusiastic applause for my liberal adversary and his witnesses, gusts of appreciative laughter for even their feeblest jokes, and roars of delight whenever one of them scored rhetorically against me—not to mention the most routine applause for my witnesses, and quite often a wave of sibilant hisses whenever I made some point of which the live audience disapproved.

I say I could "count on" all this—and I did, not at all gloomily. For I know these *manifestations de gauche* would merely outrage the far larger and more moderate audience out there beyond the cameras, whose vengeance would take the highly practical form of voting my way when the moderator, at the end of the program, asked them to vote. I therefore bore these annoying displays patiently, knowing that in due course the rural vote, so to speak, would come in.

As a matter of fact—and this brings up an interesting point about radio and TV—one problem was that the hisses, unlike the applause and laughter (or lack of them), tended not to be noticed at all by a television viewer. The sound of hissing simply wasn't picked up or transmitted well by the electronic apparatus.

That is just one of the curious modifications that television reproduction imposes on what actually occurs at the scene of a TV broadcast. Another is summed up in the expression, "The tube cools." That is to say, a very hot argument—perhaps much too hot, in the opinion of those on the spot—will appear a good deal "cooler" when reproduced on the screen of a TV set. Why this should be so is something I haven't figured out, but it is a fact for which I have been profoundly grateful on those occasions when I have let my unruly temper get somewhat too much the better of me in the course of a televised argument.

The existence of a large invisible audience is not, however, the only feature of arguing on radio or television which heightens the importance of factors that are already important in any argument. The careful selection and definition of the *topic* is (or would be, if it were possible) even more important in the case of a broadcast argument than in an ordinary one. For it will usually be announced in advance in the newspapers, if they report the affair, and people may therefore have a day or a week in which to mull it over and reach a tentative conclusion before hearing either side of the case.

Again, the matter of sequence, and especially who speaks last, is if anything even more important than usual when an argument is being broadcast. Last impressions tend to be the most powerful—especially where, as in the case of "The Advocates," the audience is being requested to *do* something: e.g., send in its votes.

Then there are those factors—like the non-transmitted hisses and "cooled" exchanges already mentioned—which are unique to the radio and television mediums. One important factor is common to them both: the pitifully short time the arguer will have in which to make his points.

Most broadcast arguments, whether on radio or TV, and whether called "panels" or "debates," are scheduled for thirty minutes. Virtually all the rest last only an hour—almost none go longer.† When time is deducted for necessary introductions and explanations, not to mention commercials if there are any, thirty minutes can shrink to fifteen or twenty with incredible ease; and when this residue is divided among (say) four panelists and two of them are talkative, an amateur can find himself fighting for even two or three minutes actually "on the air."

Even an hour, which is almost unimaginably luxurious by talk-show standards, can dwindle alarmingly. On "The Advocates," introductions (there were no commercials, of course, on PBS) and opening and closing statements by the moderator consumed eight minutes. The remaining fifty-two were divided between the two sides, twenty-six minutes apiece. But thirteen of a side's twenty-six minutes were given over to cross-examination of the opposing witnesses, leaving just thirteen minutes for the entire presentation of one's affirmative case. Since the advocate himself had to make an opening statement of up to two minutes, and summarize his case at the end of the show in sixty seconds, that gave him only ten minutes in which to take two or even three witnesses through their testimony: three to

† Among the rare exceptions, in my experience, were various all-night radio "talk shows" I participated in back in the early and mid-1960s. It was not uncommon for Long John Nebel to pit me against some suitable adversary when he came on WOR at midnight and let us belabor each other, with minimal refereeing, till 5:30 A.M. I doubt anybody was listening, but it was great training!

five minutes per witness! And these, mind you, were quite often United States senators, or professors with towering reputations in their fields, or experts flown in from abroad. Since a question and a reply of reasonable length together ordinarily consume about a minute, asking a witness more than three basic questions was often impossible.

Bear in mind, then, that your time actually "on the air" is *invariably* going to be, not merely less than you might think, but wildly, absurdly less. Pick your points, therefore, with care, concentrating on the big ones and omitting side issues, and then make them at once, as forcefully as you can. I have seen an inexperienced arguer almost totally foreclosed from the discussion by having the moderator say, "I'm sorry but our time is up" before the poor devil even got around to making his basic point.

With a little experience it is often possible, in an informal panel discussion on radio or television, to follow the time cues being given to the moderator by the stage director and intervene just in time to have that always-useful "last word." Once on the "Dick Cavett Show" I was jousting with Jane Fonda's friend Donald Sutherland over her pro-Hanoi antics, and timed as the very last comment a contemptuous reference to her habit of wearing "a tooth of Ho Chi Minh's on a necklace." Actually I knew that what she wore was a piece of metal salvaged from a U.S. bomber shot down over North Vietnam, but I had playfully chosen "a tooth of Ho Chi Minh's" as about equally offensive from an American standpoint and rather more comical. Sutherland, however, decided to be deeply offended by my remark, declaring (while the television audience was watching a commercial) that "This is exactly the sort of thing that conservatives are always doing," and begging Cavett for a chance to respond on the air. To my delight, Cavett was unable to oblige him: When the commercial was over, there was only time for Cavett's own thanks to his guests, and the sign-off. Sutherland's face was a study in frustration.

In one important respect television and radio differ sharply. On radio, one listens to the speaker. If two people are talking at once (as sometimes happens, in a hot argument), the listener hears nothing but unintelligible noise. If the same thing happens on television, however, the viewer hears clearly the speaker *whom the camera is on,* and the other talker is merely a minor background distraction.

In the case of radio this places a powerful weapon in the hand of anybody who knows the above rule, and in the case of television it puts an equally powerful weapon in the hand of the director, who can decide which of the two speakers to favor.

Of course, knowing how to make an unintelligible hash of your opponent's statements in a radio broadcast (by talking at the same time) is not the same thing as doing so; it is a weapon that ought to be used sparingly and scrupulously. Once, however, I was deeply grateful that I knew how to use it, and I used it to maximum effect.

It was in the course of a radio debate on Rhodesia with John Malecela, who was then Tanzania's ambassador to the UN. The moderator was John K. M. McCaffrey, and he was being extremely careful to give Ambassador Malecela and myself equal time to state our views. Unfortunately, the ambassador's years at the UN had accustomed him to speaking whenever he felt like it and for as long as he wished, on the serene assumption that no one would dare interrupt him. So as soon as I tried to make some point or other, Ambassador Malecela would simply interrupt and begin responding, or making some point of his own. I decided very quickly, after just two or three experiences of this tactic, that I could not afford to permit it; so I invoked The Weapon. The next time Ambassador Malecela rumbled into action in the middle of one of my sentences I began a loud and repetitious but thoroughly effective litany: "No, Mr. Ambassador, you are not going to interrupt me; I will not permit it; I will have my say and then you can have yours; no, I shall not permit this interruption"—while, of course, the ambassador too pushed doggedly on. The audience heard nothing but a wild cacophony—but at least Malecela did not get a single point in edgewise. At last McCaffrey managed to silence the ambassador; I quit talking too; and McCaffrey told Malecela, quite rightly, that it was Mr. Rusher's turn to speak and that he would then have his. The ambassador subsided grumpily, McCaffrey said, "Mr. Rusher, the floor is yours," I responded with a highly formal "*Thank* you"—and proceeded.

Next day I got a phone call from a diplomatic friend at the UN: "Mr. Rusher, you are the toast of the UN today!"

"Good Lord! You don't mean they agreed with me?"

"Certainly not! But you are the first person who ever silenced Ambassador Malecela!"

Of course, if the debate had been on TV, my triumph (or failure) would have been squarely in the hands of the director, because the audience would have heard and understood whichever of us he chose to focus the camera on.

One last point, applicable only to television, and that is the matter of makeup. Television cameras, and therefore TV directors, are getting less skittish than they used to be about white shirts and the consequent importance of "television blue," etc., but powerful Klieg lights still can and often do bleach out a healthy complexion. That is why television pros invariably use pancake makeup, and I counsel anybody who wants to look reasonably healthy, let alone competitive, on TV to overcome any *macho* qualms he may have on the subject and use it too—in fact, request it if it isn't offered. (I have known more than one television interviewer to discourage his guests from getting made up—apparently so that he, under a pound of pancake makeup, could look vigorous and brimming with tawny good health, while everybody else on the show appeared to be in the last stages of tuberculosis.)

And while we are on the subject of makeup, don't forget the matter of hands. All of us gesture with our hands, bringing them to or near our face every now and then, and if the face is made up and the hands aren't, we will end up like the famous TV talk-show star who regularly neglects this important detail and is forever resting a white, fishlike hand against his normal-seeming face. Hand makeup consists of simply brushing pancake makeup over the backs of the hands as far down as the wrists. If you care enough to argue, why not let art and science do what they can do to help you win?

ARGUING WITH POLITICIANS

Arguing publicly with politicians is an art involving considerations so special that it deserves a section all its own.

As a group, politicians are dangerously knowledgeable, articulate, and slippery, and the average person is well advised to steer clear of arguing with them altogether. The time may come, however, when arguing with some politician is unavoidable. Alternatively, you may just want to try your luck. If so, be of good heart: Politicians have special vulnerabilities as well as special strengths.

First though, remember those strengths. Almost any politician worthy of the name will know a good deal—in all likelihood more than you do—about public affairs in general and matters involving his bailiwick in particular. The town selectman will be full of information on the new sewer bond issue; the mayor will drown you in statistics about the police department budget, etc. At the congressional level you will be dealing with what amounts to a walking newspaper; and in addition every congressman is a member of several committees and subcommittees dealing with particular subjects (defense, agriculture, the post office, what-have-you), on which he is quite often a real expert. (And therefore must be dealt with, at least in part, like any other expert.) As for United States Senators, their knowledge and skills are frequently even greater than those of Congressmen, from whose ranks they are so often recruited by Darwinian processes.

In addition, politicians are almost by definition highly articulate. Ordinarily they have gotten where they are by cultivating a special knack for putting things the way lots of people like to hear them. Besides, practice makes perfect: The constant speechifying hones their oratorical skills. They learn, by sheer trial and error, which appeals work and which don't and how best to put every point. Perhaps most important of all, they "know where the bodies are buried"—i.e., what the *really* difficult questions are. And they will have prepared careful answers for those questions as well as for the easier ones.

It is safest to assume that there is no subject on which your information is superior to the politician's (unless, of course, you are lucky enough to have some real blockbuster for him) and that he will have anticipated, and have smooth answers for, most of the conventionally difficult questions you can ask him. Your task, then, is to find some loose brick in his facade—some dilemma in which he will be damned if he does and damned if he doesn't.‡ And that brings us to the matter of a politician's special vulnerabilities.

‡ For a stellar example of such a dilemma, see the question I confected for Bill Buckley to ask Nixon—p. 98.

Since the job of a politician is to amass as much support for himself as possible, he is forever trying to win the backing of various blocs that disagree with each other. ("There are two points of view on everything," as the saying goes. "If you want to be popular, take both.") When he has succeeded in doing so, however (and it is remarkable how easily some skillful politicians can achieve this), he must then take care not to be caught agreeing with one bloc of his supporters on some point that is anathema to another bloc. In practice this means that he must cultivate an ability to sound forthright while using expressions that are actually capable of two or even more quite separate interpretations.

Thus the Republican party's nationwide slogan in the off-year Congressional elections of 1946 was, "Had enough? Vote Republican." The beauty of this, of course, lay in its masterly ambiguity. It didn't matter what the voter had "had enough" of; if he was fed up about anything at all, the slogan sounded as if it was aimed squarely at him. (The same was true of the popular cry in the recent film, *The Network:* "I'm mad as hell and I'm not going to take it anymore!") The voters rewarded the GOP by giving it control of Congress for two of the only four years during which it has enjoyed control in the past half century.

Or consider the felicity of Kevin White's basic slogan when he ran for mayor, with a record as a liberal on race issues, in racially troubled Boston: "VOTE WHITE FOR MAYOR." How many votes was that worth, do you suppose, in Southie?

My very favorite, though, was a large newspaper ad published shortly before Election Day by a committee of John Lindsay's supporters, when Hizzoner was running for reelection in 1969. The committee was ethnically and religiously well balanced, as such committees must be in polyglot New York. But the bold-type question that headed and dominated the ad was a beauty: "WHY IS THIS ELECTION DIFFERENT FROM ALL OTHER ELECTIONS?" The answer, as given in the ad, was that it offered voters a golden opportunity to reelect a man who . . . etc., etc. Practically no one but Jewish voters (but all of the latter) recognized the headline as a close paraphrase of the question that the youngest male child in every Orthodox Jewish family asks of the family patriarch on the first night of Passover: "Why is

this night different from all other nights?" In the New York *Post*,
which was at that time perhaps the favorite newspaper of New
York's two million Jews, Lindsay was blowing that community a special kiss—a gesture invisible, moreover, to everyone else. (If a committee supporting his Republican opponent John Marchi had run an
ad in the *Daily News* headed "ONWARD MARCHI SOLDIERS!" there
would have been hell to pay. Some gestures are more obvious, and
therefore more offensive, than others.)

Ambiguity, then, is of the very essence of democratic politics. Ordinarily it will take the form of concealing the fact that a politician's
current allegiances are, to a greater or lesser degree, inconsistent. But
it may also be used to conceal the difference between the position a
politician took yesterday and the one he is taking today. Finally, it
has all sorts of collateral functions: concealing the gaps between a
politician's promises and his performance; between his party's platform and his own statements; between his running mate and himself; etc.

In arguing with a politician it is seldom possible to overwhelm
him with masses of facts or overawe him with appeals to principle,
but he can sometimes be forced to confront and clarify the ambigui-
ties in his position. If this is successfully done (and it is usually no
easy job), he will ordinarily have only three choices: (1) to come
down on your side of the question (reluctantly, to be sure, since
doing so will cost him support on the other side—as Nixon gloomily
realized); (2) to come down on the other side of the question
(equally reluctantly), in which case he will alienate those on your
side of the controversy; or (3) to insist, despite everything, on his
shield of ambiguity—in which case he will be perceived by the audience, correctly, as a weaseler.

That mention of the audience, incidentally, brings up an important point: There is almost no use arguing with a politician (on a
public issue, that is) unless an audience is present, at least deriva-
tively: e.g., when he is talking to a reporter "on the record." When
he knows his privacy is guaranteed, a politician is far more relaxed:
He can say whatever he feels like saying, knowing that his statements
will not become a part of the record and thus cannot be held against
him. Under such circumstances he may be far more entertaining,

and also more informative, but he will be almost impossible to hold to any given view. Before an audience he will be a totally different person, at least as far as responsibility for his utterances is concerned.

I had this brought home to me once when I was invited to audition as the possible host of a talk-show that New York City's Channel 5 (WNEW-TV) was planning to produce. My "guest" (and prospective victim) on the audition show was to be County Executive (now federal judge) Eugene Nickerson of Nassau County, whom Channel 5 had lured into the role by leaving him under the impression that the show probably would, or at least might, be broadcast. Being under the same impression myself, I prepared a series of questions which I hoped it would be difficult for Mr. Nickerson, as a practicing politician, to answer forthrightly in public. When we arrived for the taping, however, and were in the makeup room having our war paint applied, one of the show's prospective producers inadvertently let slip the deadly news that this was, in fact, a pure dry run. To me this mattered very little, but to Nickerson it was all-important. He verified his understanding of the situation with a careful question—and then, when the cameras rolled, answered my toughest questions with the zesty nonchalance of a man who knew he had nothing to lose. He enjoyed the occasion, as he had every right to—and, incidentally, also made a hash of my hopes of landing the contract as host!

Their knowledge of their special vulnerability makes most able politicians extremely wary of being trapped in situations where it— and they—can be exposed. They love to make speeches at Lincoln Day dinners and similar functions where the risks are zero and approval is guaranteed; but they frequently have a conflicting engagement if the invitation to speak runs any risk of exposing the speaker to some really tough arguing.

I once saw the late State Senator Earl Brydges of Niagara Falls, New York, ensnared in a genuine debate with an able opponent when he had probably expected a taffy-pull, and his fury afterward was memorable. It was about 1958, and *National Review* was sponsoring a series of debates on public issues at the Hunter College Auditorium in Manhattan. On the evening in question the topic was, "Should the Republican Party Repudiate Eisenhower?"—a proposal that, if he was told about it at all before reaching the auditorium, must have struck Senator Brydges as the absolute last word in preposterousness. He had been recruited to defend President Eisenhower through the good offices of the Speakers Bureau of the Republican State Committee in Albany, to which we had turned for a speaker, and undoubtedly looked forward to a real pushover.

Unfortunately for him these debates were attended largely by friends and supporters of *National Review* who were as exasperated by Eisenhower's deft political ambiguity as we on the magazine were, and their spokesman that evening, and thus Brydges' opponent, was the late Willmoore Kendall, the NR columnist and noted political scientist, who was one of the ablest and wittiest debaters I have ever heard. Kendall delighted the audience with his sallies, e.g., accusing Eisenhower of "descending with the speed of a guided missile to what I can only call the Zasu Pitts level of political oratory." The crowd roared its approval. Brydges commendably kept his cool, but he was forgivably miserable over the situation, and I later received a first-hand account of a blistering phone call Brydges made immediately afterward to the Republican Speakers Bureau, laying it out in lavender for steering him into such an ambush.

Fortunately for politicians there are various conventions, or understandings, that tend to protect them. For one thing, two senators (say) will rarely go after each other hammer-and-tongs even though, or more precisely because, each usually has enough on the other—understands well enough the concealed inconsistencies in his adversary's position—to give him a very rough time. A public argument between two politicians, therefore, is quite likely to be a rather guarded affair. It may be partly a matter of "senatorial courtesy"—but what, after all, is senatorial courtesy if not a tacit mutual agreement to stop short of trying to injure one another too deeply?

By the same token the Sunday television talk shows like "Meet the Press" expose the politician-guest to a considerable amount of potentially deadly radiation, but the political reporters on the panel—assuming they aren't in the politician's corner to begin with, and therefore merely trying to make him look good—are aware that they must live with, and to some extent on, these politicians they are questioning, and therefore they rarely go all the way to the jugular.

In fairness, one should acknowledge that politicians are more vulnerable than most of us not only because they tend to be inconsistent but because their very careers and livelihoods may depend—as ours do not—upon their responses. A private citizen, engaged in a free-swinging debate with a congressman, may be able to adopt a provocative stance without risking any disapproval more damaging than his brother-in-law's; but the congressman may be laying his job on the line. However, as John Kennedy observed, life is unfair; and besides, nobody asked the congressman to run for the job. He is fair game, therefore, to the extent that he can be brought to bay.

Unfortunately, for the reasons already discussed, there are fewer opportunities than one might suppose, or than there ought to be, to tree a competent politician. Most of those from a typically mixed constituency for example, will assert, when pressed, that they simply don't *know* whether they are liberal or conservative (or alternatively will declare stoutly that they dislike such arbitrary "labeling"). They are also dead set against "one-issue voters" (i.e., voters whose support or opposition depends upon the politician's position on a single issue)—naturally, since such singlemindedness makes it impossible for them to satisfy important blocs of voters with half a loaf. ("I'm hard on defense and fiscal matters and soft on welfare," Nelson Rockefeller used to wail—privately—to conservatives. "You've got two thirds of me. What more do you want?")

Nonetheless the day occasionally dawns when a politician finds himself in a position to be questioned sharply in public (or on the record) by someone not so vulnerable as himself. We have already mentioned one such instance—Bill Buckley's interview with then-Vice-President Nixon back in 1957 (p. 98). For another, let us turn to my cross-examination of two leading politicians, Congressman Morris Udall and former Attorney General Ramsey Clark, on a 1970 "Advocates" program where the topic was, "Should the federal government register voters for presidential elections?"

The proposal that citizens be encouraged to vote by making it easier for them to register—in fact, by registering them in a door-to-door canvass conducted by federal employees—is one of those superficially appealing suggestions that are difficult to oppose without sounding merely hidebound. ("Do you want to keep people from voting?") One of my own witnesses in opposition to the proposal, Senator Peter Dominick (R., Colorado), had bravely agreed to be on the show despite his own gloomy conviction that there was "no way to win" the vote of the TV audience.

I was less pessimistic. For one thing, sober reflection would quickly convince any thoughtful person that the effect of such a law would be to register precisely those potential voters who are the least informed and most indifferent: not really a very good advertisement for the supposed glories of the democratic political process. For another, the bill which was to be the centerpiece of the discussion, and which had been introduced in the House of Representatives by Congressman Udall at the behest of the Democratic National Committee (where it had actually been drafted), was a very poorly designed affair. Looking over a copy, I discovered that one provision actually made registration not merely easy but compulsory, and that another would make the list of registered voters so compiled available for any purpose whatever (and that apparently included commercial purposes) to any state or local election official who requested it.

Now, those were serious criticisms of the bill as introduced by Udall, and I was sure they would weigh against it in the eyes of a good many liberals with libertarian instincts or with even the natural and widespread aversion to the current overuse of mailing lists. No doubt the flaws would be dismissed by the other side as correctible trivia, but they were undeniably in the bill before us, and Congressman Udall was proudly presented to viewers by his own side as the man who had introduced the bill. So I wasted no time confronting this able politician with the gulf between what his bill proposed and what I was sure would be his own decent instincts. The effect was to make Udall (who after all had actually introduced the bill largely as a favor to the Democratic National Committee) look rather ridiculous:

RUSHER: "Congressman Udall, I presume that there would, under almost any system, be some people who chose, however, not to vote?"

UDALL: "Doubtless."

RUSHER: "And not to register even if they had the choice?"

UDALL: "Indeed."

RUSHER: "Now, what about those people under your bill?"

UDALL: "The philosophy of my bill, Mr. Rusher, is simply that we give them a chance. We give them an opportunity. If they reject that chance, so be it. But most of the people who are shut out today are shut out involuntarily."

RUSHER: "The statement that you inserted in the Congressional Record when you introduced the bill stated that 'the bill would enroll every qualified person to vote who does not refuse.'"

UDALL: "Well, this has been unfortunate language, of which there is considerable in the Congressional Record. (laughter) The intention of the bill is simply to give them an opportunity to vote, Mr. Rusher."

RUSHER: "The intention of the bill is indeed that; but in point of fact it compels them to register, does it not, and there isn't a word in your bill from one end to the other that says a thing about it being voluntary?"

UDALL: "I think that there's a question of interpretation here."

RUSHER: "I hand you your bill and ask you to tell us where it says it's voluntary."

UDALL: "Well, this is a ten-page bill . . ."

RUSHER: "Take your time." (laughter)

At this point I had poor Udall thumbing haplessly through "his" bill, looking desperately for a liberating provision that I knew, and he by this time at least darkly suspected, wasn't there. He kept up a little patter while he hunted:

UDALL: "I shall be glad to find you the provision. It's intended to give them the opportunity to register but not require them to register. And I would simply say that if the technical language would be interpreted by lawyers to require them to register, we can correct that with an amendment, which I would support."

RUSHER: "It can be interpreted by anybody who reads English."

Finally I ended his misery:

RUSHER: ". . . I refer you to line 3 of page 4: 'When every such determination has been made with respect to any person'—that is, the determination that he is qualified—'his name *shall* [emphasis Rusher's] be entered on an enrollment roll compiled by the national enrollment officials for the election district concerned.'"

Udall saw my point, and adopted evasive tactics, not very successfully:

UDALL: "Yes. But there's nothing in the bill that would require that person so enrolled, to go down and vote. No one's going to haul him to . . ."

RUSHER: "I didn't say it did. But it does require him to register and for his name to be on the list, doesn't it?"

UDALL: "It puts his name on a list which will permit him to vote . . ."

RUSHER: "Whether he likes it or not."

UDALL: "Whether he likes it or not; and he can reject that opportunity."

I then proceeded to my second objection:

RUSHER: "Now let's see what happens to that list. What happens to the list, Congressman?"

UDALL: "Well, the list goes to the election officials on the election day, and if that individual shows up, he can demand the right to vote for his President . . ."

RUSHER: "And after Election Day, what happens to the list?"

UDALL: "The list is destroyed unless the state officials want that list for their own purposes."

RUSHER: "And if they do?"

UDALL: "They get the list."

RUSHER: "In other words, any state or local official who asks for the list gets it, is that correct?"

UDALL: "Not any state official but those in charge of . . ."

RUSHER: "State or local *election* official."

UDALL: "Precisely."

RUSHER: "That's correct. And they can get it without any restrictions on use whatever."

UDALL: "No, indeed. We hope they'll use it."

RUSHER: "Show me the restrictions on their use of it."

Udall's "No indeed" had been intended to deny my contention that there were no restrictions on the use of the list, though he added that "We hope they'll use it,"—i.e., to get those registered to come out and vote. Now he was thumbing through the bill again, looking for some restriction that would prevent an election official from simply selling such a list to a direct-mail house. I couldn't resist teasing him gently:

UDALL: "I don't know whether there are adequate restrictions in the bill as now written . . ."

RUSHER: "Did you read the bill before you introduced it?"

UDALL: "Oh, I did, indeed." (laughter)

RUSHER: "Did you draft it?"

UDALL: "Line by line, word by word."

RUSHER: "Well, are there any words that say that the list cannot be used for any purpose whatever by the local official who takes it?"

Udall threw in the sponge:

UDALL: "No, but I would be glad to write such a restriction."

RUSHER: "I'm sure you would. I daresay you wish you had." (laughter)

A little later it was the turn of former Attorney General Ramsey Clark. He had listened to the ordeal of Congressman Udall, and was determined not to get mired in the unfortunate details of the Udall bill. I was, of course, equally determined to mire him there. He ended his direct testimony with a rousing peroration, but I was able to elide smoothly from it to my chief point:

CLARK: ". . . Political power in America has got to be shared with all of our people, and there's only one way to do it, and that's to go to the people and say please educate yourself. Please inform yourself. Please register. Please be enrolled and vote. We need you."

PALMIERI: "Mr. Clark, on that note, let me introduce to you Mr. William Rusher who has some questions on cross examination."

RUSHER: "Good evening, Mr. Clark."

CLARK: "Good evening, sir."

RUSHER: "You want to say 'please' to these people. Does the bill say 'please'?"

CLARK: "Well, the bill *can* say 'please,' can't it? Do we want to stick on the central issue, purpose of this bill or do you want to stick on the details?"

RUSHER: "I want to stick on the bill. Do you want to get away from it?"

CLARK: "I'm prepared to get away from it. I want the best bill we can get."

RUSHER: "I'll bet you are. But I want to stay with it. The topic to-night is the bill, Mr. Clark, and if you don't mind we'll discuss that."

Clark was a fighter, and by now he was on warning that I was one too, and he quite properly insisted on hanging in there for "the prin-ciple" of universal voter registration, whatever Udall's unfortunate bill might say. I, in turn, brought up another defect in the bill:

RUSHER: "How about under Mr. Udall's bill, which you're here to defend, the national enrollment director appointing 435 district di-rectors without the slightest provision that there should be anything bi-partisan about his choice?"

CLARK: "There can be bi-partisanism. Even more than that, we need a dozen checks."

RUSHER: "I'm aware that there can be, but is there any requirement that there must be?"

CLARK: "I think there are ample checks and we know . . ."

RUSHER: "What ample checks are there?"

CLARK: "Well, you're talking about the bill again."

RUSHER: "You're talking about the checks. Where are they?"

CLARK: "I would like to talk about what's possible."

RUSHER: "I want to talk about the ample checks that you say exist in the bill."

CLARK: "You talk about what you want to talk about, and I'll talk about what I want to talk about." (laughter)

RUSHER: "All right. You don't want to talk about it."

CLARK: "I want to talk about what's possible. I think America has to address itself to real problems and not puny technicalities. And the real problem here is getting the people to vote here, and you can do it. You can have ample checks."

Yes, but the Udall bill didn't contain them, and when the TV au-dience's votes were counted I was able to phone Senator Dominick with the gratifying news that we had achieved a flat tie: 48 percent to 48 percent, with 4 percent expressing "other views."

So politicians *can* be debated, when necessary.

HOW TO COPE WITH A HOSTILE AUDIENCE

Audiences come in all sizes and moods, from the oral examiners of a candidate for a Ph.D. to participants in a giant political rally. In the case of a debate or other argument, the audience is usually to be wooed and won—though exceptions to this rule are not rare. (In a college debate, for example, the "target" may be three official judges, whose conclusion may differ widely from that of the larger audience.)

Assuming the general audience is the target, what if it is hostile? In extreme cases, of course, nothing can be done, and it is ridiculous even to try. In certain other situations, the speaker may deliberately choose not to try to avert audience hostility, preferring for reasons of either principle or strategy to stand his ground—and lose. But frequently it is possible for an arguer before a hostile audience to persuade the audience, if not of the correctness of his views, at least that he is sincere in holding them, and thus that he is to that degree deserving of the audience's respect. Once that much has been established, it is sometimes possible to persuade at least a part of the audience to take further steps: from respect to sympathy, and from sympathy to support. This, roughly, is the miracle that Shakespeare has Mark Antony perform on the Roman mob that assembled in the Forum after Caesar's assassination. In real life it is seldom or never possible to change an audience's made-up mind as swiftly and completely as Shakespeare's Antony does; but the principle is valid and partial successes are not infrequent.

As mentioned earlier, I used roughly that technique to obtain a standing ovation from a hostile audience at Berkeley in the latter half of the 1960s, during a debate on the Vietnam war. I had, to put it mildly, the unpopular side of the issue, at least in terms of public opinion at Berkeley. I particularly remember that the front row, where some of the noisiest peaceniks were sitting, positively seethed with hostility. (Ever since, I have been fond of telling my friends, "You haven't lived until you've seen the front row at Berkeley!")

Perhaps, however, that front row was my salvation. I am not generally much inclined to give way before a hostile audience reaction, preferring to defy it or laugh at it unless for some reason I deeply need the audience's support. But I adopted, that day at Berkeley, a defensive stance of modest earnestness that made that front row's conduct seem excessive to their colleagues farther back—which proves, I guess, that audiences are human too.

An *individual* heckler in an American audience can generally be treated as a special case analogous to Berkeley's front row: I.e., he will more often than not, and especially if he is persistent, turn the audience against himself and in favor of the speaker. This is much less true in Britain, where heckling by opposition members is a feature of debates in the House of Commons that has been carried over to public platforms and makes heckling during a British political address much commoner and more acceptable than it is here. An English debater or speaker in any political context is ordinarily expected to answer hecklers—preferably by putting them down wittily. ("How many toes on a pig's foot?" a Labour heckler once shouted at Nancy Astor, implying that the aristocratic Tory M.P. wouldn't know about such plebeian fare. "Why don't you take off your boots and count 'em?" she snapped back—winning game, set, and match.)

To be sure, coping with a hostile audience is a task best left to people who feel reasonably at home in front of the public; it is hardly recommended for people who suffer from stage fright and have trouble enough appearing before a friendly audience, let alone a hostile one. But never let it be said that there is no hope if the audience is hostile.

Of course, the wrong move can be fatal. A Boston friend once told me of a candidate for Attorney General of Massachusetts in the Democratic primary who, on being booed during a campaign debate, challenged anybody in the audience who thought he was lying to come up on the platform and say so, face to face. "The entire audience," my friend said, chuckling, "rose as one man and advanced upon the platform!"

XII

MANNERS OF SPEAKING

It may have surprised some readers that I have come this far in a book about argumentation without yet saying anything very magisterial about the matter of *style:* that indefinable element in any argument that concerns, not *what* is said, but *how* it is said. Certainly my silence was not intended to imply that style is unimportant; on the contrary, a careful and intelligent choice of how to put an argument can often be decisive.

In part, however, my reticence has been due to a deep conviction that important as style may be, it is not, or at any rate ought not to be, so important as substance: A good argument can make its way in the world, and reasonably hope to prevail, even if the opposition is stylistically superior. A great many inept arguers sincerely believe they lose their arguments because their opponents are "smooth" or "a good talker" or obscurely "slick," when the truth is that they lose because their opponents have chosen their stands with greater care and defended them with better arguments, any superiority in style being merely the frosting on the cake. "Be good, sweet maid, and let who will be clever" was not originally intended as advice to arguers, and may be a little treacly for some tastes, but it isn't far off the mark. If you ever have to choose between solid substance and mere flashy style, by all means choose the substance and let who will choose the style. Like honesty, reliance on substance is (in addition to everything else) the best "policy."

Another reason for my diffidence about going deeply into the matter of style is the fact that it is such a large and easily separable subject that it really belongs in another book: a book on what used to be called "elocution," or more broadly "rhetoric." We are not all

equally gifted by nature in these respects, and happily it is possible
for someone who feels inadequate in them to improve his or her performance markedly by study and hard work. But it is a very broad
subject, and in a book that is basically about argumentation it will
not be possible to do more than point down some of the more obvious roads. Anyone who is conscious of shortcomings as a speaker,
however (and that includes most people), will do well to consult a
book or enroll in a course on that subject.

One final major problem with discussing style is that it is such an
intensely personal matter that it is difficult to generalize about it. No
two people are alike, and what works superbly well for Jones may
sound positively ludicrous when tried by Smith. Any "rule" I might
propound in this field would be instantly vulnerable to the response
that some towering expert has violated it repeatedly. One arguer may
often contrive to suggest that the point he wants to make actually
originated with you. Another may be adept at implying that all
men of good will naturally agree with him. Yet another may succeed
in shaking you loose from some cherished conviction by successfully
demonstrating, over your dead body, that it is absurd. One person
may specialize in winning you over by seeming to appeal for your
help; another may excite your admiration so powerfully that you
want to rush to his banner. All of those devices, and a thousand
others as well, have been used successfully many times; but it is impossible to say who ought to use which, and who should not. These
various devices are comfortable or uncomfortable, depending on the
persona of the individual. As a practical matter we tend to learn by
trial and error, long before we reach maturity, which work best for
us.

Years ago I dated a girl who, when asked if she would like to go to
some particular favorite restaurant, had a way of widening her eyes
and answering with "Yes?"—"yes" *asked as a question*. The rising in-
tonation suggested that she liked the idea so much she didn't quite
dare to risk a flat affirmative. It was not "Yes, definitely!" but "Yes,
may I really?"—a very charming little trick. I often thought that it
was probably invented for, and practiced to perfection on, a doting
father when she was only three or four. (It also melted me.)

A great trick—but not necessarily recommended for everyone!

Still, a few observations on style—on how an argument ought to be put—certainly belong in any book on argumentation. And the first of them is that considerations of style are every bit as important in informal arguments as they are in the most formal debates. The tone of voice, for example, in which an argument is put forward often has an enormous amount to do with whether the audience will accept it —and this is as true if the audience is one's wife as it is if it is an entire auditorium full of people. Devoting a little thought to how to put your case almost always pays.

Let us stay with that matter of tone of voice for a moment, since it is by far the most important aspect of style; it also conveys most of the others. Sincerity is always highly appreciated by an American audience (whereas a British audience may value wit as highly, or even more highly), and should ordinarily be conveyed by one's tone of voice. But sincerity is often not enough. The arguer must also give evidence—preferably indirect, in the interests of modesty—of knowing what he is talking about. A tone of authority can be conveyed by a relaxed manner (always taking care not to be so relaxed as to appear contemptuous), by an evident thoughtfulness and precision in stating one's conclusions, and by the ease with which relevant material, especially factual material, is handled.

Earnestness too, which adds to sincerity an element of eagerness, is a useful quality to convey by one's tone of voice—provided the earnestness is on behalf of an objective with which the audience is known to sympathize. (Earnestness on behalf of some objective the audience is unsure about may merely convince it that the arguer is too emotional on the subject to be trusted.)

Courtesy in argumentation no doubt ought to be taken for granted, but—these days at least—it is sufficiently often lacking to require mention. It too is, at least in part, demonstrated by one's tone of voice. The necessary assumption in almost every argument is that, however wrong he may be, one's opponent's points are worth at least *prima facie* examination. If they aren't—if your opponent is too frivolous, or too stupid, or too evil to listen to—then you shouldn't be arguing with him at all. It is theoretically conceivable that one might undertake to argue with somebody purely for the purpose of enlightening him, without making any concession whatever to the possibility that his current position may have some validity; but any arguer who conveys that impression is likely to succeed only in annoying the audience if there is one, not to mention his adversary.

Courtesy, then, requires one to listen to one's opponent for a reasonable time, and to keep interruptions (if they are allowed at all) to a decent minimum. Personally, I have always found this latter piece of advice extremely hard to follow. I am a born interrupter—not, I hasten to say, because I *want* to be discourteous, but because my mind has raced ahead of the point my adversary has just made to some crushing response that I find it unbearably difficult to delay.

Before the reader condemns me too extravagantly, let me point out that under certain circumstances the temptation to interrupt, and even the justification for doing so, is far more powerful than the audience may suspect. On "The Advocates," for example, it was quite common for a "witness" to filibuster deliberately to a certain extent, on the theory that as long as he was talking the advocate cross-examining him wasn't getting anywhere. When you have only six minutes in which to cross-examine an able witness, and directly behind his back (but out of sight of the camera) a stage director is giving you silent cues as to how much time you have left (two minutes— one minute—thirty seconds), it is almost unendurably aggravating to have the witness embark on a third or fourth illustration of some point you could counter easily if you could only get a word in edgewise.

Still, it is (in this case) the audience whose perception dominates, and the audience needs at least a brief time to digest the other side's point before hearing the riposte. It therefore actively resents an interrupter who insists upon tailgating his adversary in this fashion. I have probably, in the course of my life, lost or damaged more arguments in this way than in any other.

Of course, there are exceptions to the rule against interruption, as to all others. "The Advocates" is not the only forum in which certain adversaries are deliberate or unwitting filibusterers, quite capable of using up (say) the entire twenty-six minutes of radio time available to a panel of four unless somebody stops them. Even in such cases, however, I ordinarily favor a well-timed short interruption (often no more than a sharply barked "Why?" or "Name one!") to anything lengthier. Stopping a really nonstop talker is the job of the moderator.

Sincerity, authority, earnestness, courtesy: These are probably the four most important elements of style that are ordinarily conveyed by tone of voice. But in addition, depending on the situation, tone of voice can also convey almost every other imaginable quality or attitude: amusement, amazement, dismay, disgust, incredulity, skepticism, outrage, pride, wistfulness, idealism, courage, exasperation. The list is endless.

If, however, tone of voice can be used to convey 90 percent of the elements of style in argumentation, it is not the only means of doing so. In these days of sharply differing personal "lifestyles," even clothing can—deliberately or otherwise—convey one's attitude toward one's adversary, or toward the argument itself, or even toward the audience. Similarly, an audience may perceive and resent evidence that an arguer has prepared his case insufficiently or not at all. My mind goes back to the debater previously described who—at any rate in my experience with him—ordinarily showed up an hour late and so woefully unprepared that he simply had to go second in order to compose, during his adversary's presentation, some remarks by way of rebuttal. I often wondered what the sponsors and audience thought of his obvious indifference to them. However, those were the high days of the "campus revolt," and the audiences were often noisily in his corner; perhaps they really didn't mind his lateness or his laziness, and he was therefore strategically on sound ground in employing them simply to annoy me!

Where an arguer is confronted with some particularly obdurate mind-set that simply must be put aside if he is to prevail, it is often useful to take the target audience into one's confidence, admit the problem, and appeal for its help in overcoming the obstacle. This was what I tried to do in my case-opener on "The Advocates" first program concerning nuclear power. One of the opposing witnesses, a Dr. John Gofman of the University of California, had recently written an alarming book about its dangers, and I moved to counter his impact:

"If I may take you into my confidence for a moment, the real problem in arguing a case like this one is its technical aspects. There is no serious question about the need for a bigger energy supply in America in the years ahead, and not even any real doubt that nuclear power plants can provide that power more cheaply and more cleanly than either coal or oil. But nuclear physics is a mystery to most of us, and we know only that nuclear radiation can, under certain circumstances, be dangerous. It is undetectable to the human senses, and yet it can kill. I'm afraid that it was all too predictable that some scientist could and would be found tonight to attack the collective judgment of virtually all the rest and to predict in firm tones, as Dr. Gofman did in his recent book, that under the present safety guidelines there could be as many as 32,000 additional deaths from cancer in America every year. What can I do with statements like that? What can I reasonably ask *you* to do with them, except to freeze all nuclear power plant construction just as Mr. Miller demands? You cannot check Dr. Gofman's data, or even his arithmetic. Even if the odds are overwhelming that he is wrong, there remains some small chance that he may be right. And common sense seems to say, play it safe. But I invite you to be a little bolder than that: to listen with me to what the representatives of the overwhelming majority of the international scientific community have to say. And then, vote for the future, for a cleaner environment, for a stronger and healthier America made possible by, and only by, the rational and intelligent use of nuclear power."

On that occasion (though not on a later one involving nuclear power) a majority of the voting viewers accepted my invitation.

One could go on indefinitely, listing tactics whereby an arguer can ingratiate himself with his audience, or even with his adversary, and call the resulting list a compendium of recommendations on style. In fact, however, we are verging here on territory mapped out long ago by Dale Carnegie and concerning at bottom the impact of a personality on its surroundings. This important factor mightily affects the outcome of many an argument, but it is not, strictly speaking, a feature of the argumentation.

XIII

ADVICE FROM A FEW
EXPERTS

While I was engaged in writing the first draft of this book, an inspired friend suggested that it would add substantially to the book's interest, and probably to its pedagogical content as well, if I could persuade half a dozen or so of my own particularly memorable adversaries to respond to a short questionnaire on, roughly, How They Do It.

No sooner said than done: I drafted ten questions, designed to elicit their innermost debating secrets, and sent them winging on their way to various friends and (dialectical) foes. A couple just didn't bother to answer; *tant pis*. Allard Lowenstein, who was busy campaigning for Kennedy when my letter reached him, was tragically killed before he could find time to reply. The rest responded nobly, and their answers are set forth below.

Several—too cautious (or perhaps just too lazy!) to answer my specific questions—submitted instead brief essays on the art of argumentation; but these were so well done that I have included them, along with my original ten questions and the answers of those who elected to answer them.

I may add that the list of people to whom I sent the questionnaire eventually included not only some of the most formidable debating adversaries with whom I have ever crossed swords, but a couple whom I personally have never debated but whose argumentative skills I have always admired. That is how Phyllis Schlafly and Senator Daniel Patrick Moynihan come to be included. If Fate ever hands me the grim assignment of debating either of them, I shall study carefully, in advance, their comments herein!

As for the rest, Howard Miller and I of course argued with each other to the point of near-stupefaction on the "Advocates" programs on PBS—about forty-five times all told, by my calculation. David Schoenbrun and I must have had nearly two thirds as many debates over the years—on various platforms around the country, once or twice on "The Advocates," and in a series of brief but intense encounters on WPIX-TV (Channel 11, New York) back in the mid-1970s. With Mike Harrington I have crossed swords repeatedly before various college audiences. Ken Galbraith I have encountered on only one public occasion, but the memory is seared on my brain. As for Pat Buchanan, since we agree on most things there have been few occasions for us to debate; but there are bystanders still alive who remember a yelling match that Pat and I engaged in over Richard Nixon in Des Moines a few years back as one of the few wholly verbal equivalents of the saloon brawls that badmen used to stage in the Old West. Pat is also held in awe by connoisseurs (as he shyly admits in the essay herein) for having made hamburger out of the entire Senate Watergate Committee when it sought to torment him.

With Bill Buckley too, our tendency to see many things alike has limited the opportunities for formal debates; but around *National Review* we have often found occasion to disagree and to say so. I can thus claim extensive personal experience of Sir William's debating style.

First, then, here are the ten questions I addressed to my correspondents:

1. Whom do you consider the three (or more, or fewer, as you prefer) most formidable arguers you have ever faced? Why (i.e., what were their respective special strengths)?
2. What do you consider the most important single factor in winning an argument? (Short- or longer-form answer, as you wish.)
3. Must a person, to be a good arguer, have a "killer instinct"?
4. Broadly speaking, would you rather speak first or last? (Or does it depend—or matter?)
5. When an arguer is caught in a mistake, what is his best course?
6. Do you think that purely rhetorical devices (as distinguished

from cogency of argumentation) play a large, medium, or small role, or none at all, in determining who wins an argument?

7. If you find yourself in an argument with a large and heavily bureaucratic organization (typically government, but corporations too), do you have any special techniques for winning?

8. What is the commonest mistake made by inexperienced arguers? (I know—"arguing." But can you be more specific?)

9. How do you handle a hostile audience?

10. Has the experience you have gained in formal arguments been useful to you in everyday personal and business life? (Cite an example, if you wish.)

I think you will find the answers of these eight black-belt arguers as fascinating as I did. The points on which they disagree are as surprising as those on which they are unanimous—and both are highly instructive.

Several of them misunderstood my seventh question—which is my fault, not theirs. They rightly understood my questionnaire as dealing largely with debates before audiences; not having seen the book, they did not recognize that I was envisioning, in question 7, a quite different type of situation.

Here, then, in alphabetical order, are the responses of those who answered the questions directly:

William F. Buckley:

1. I find it extremely difficult to name the three most formidable arguers I have ever faced. The reason for this is that circumstances so frequently dictate the strength of a speaker—the crowd, the occasion, the mission, that kind of thing. With these qualifiers, I would name Sidney Hook, Michael Harrington, and Carey McWilliams, Jr. Sidney's strength is his ability to proceed along a logical sequence resulting in rhetorically explosive accumulative effects. Michael's strength is in preempting virtue, concern, plus a kind of rugged, boyish appeal to the audience. Carey McWilliams is a master of the forensic art who gives in just enough to his opponent to appease a crowd that might otherwise be reluctant to desert the alternative position.

2. The most important single factor in winning an argument is appraising the mood and desires of the audience.

3. No, a person in order to be a good arguer need not have a killer instinct. On the contrary, my experience, with one or two exceptions, leads me to conclude that a killer instinct can hurt in that it engenders sympathy for the opponent.

4. Would I rather speak first or last? It very definitely depends. If I anticipate that there will be a great confusion in respect to the issues, I like to speak first, so that I can plant my positions with care. The disadvantage of speaking first as far as I'm concerned is that I am uncomfortable doing so extemporaneously. The advantages of speaking last are manifest—there is no one around to answer your rhetoric. I have both won and lost debates as a result of the last statement.

5. When an arguer is caught in a mistake his best course of action is to trivialize its significance.

6. Rhetorical devices play a significant part always, not so much in winning an argument, but in winning over the audience. An important distinction. A lousy argument can take over the house if the rhetoric is effectively fashioned.

7. The most effective device in front of a large organization is to praise it. I regularly, indeed almost religiously, set out to lose the audience in such circumstances (i.e., I make fun of it, and decline to kiss its posterior), seeking other satisfactions.

8. Inexperienced arguers tend to make over-complicated points, repeat themselves, tend to diffuseness, miss altogether subtleties of analysis, are easily flustered, and go on too long. Needless to say, not all inexperienced arguers suffer these disabilities simultaneously, but from the list almost any inexperienced arguer would borrow.

9. I handle a hostile audience by an intentionally cold indifference to its feelings toward me. More often than not, a few will then reach out to touch my hand.

10. My general feeling is that skill in formal argument hurts one in personal and business life, in that it encourages adversary postures where conciliatory postures are indicated.

Michael Harrington:

1. William F. Buckley, Jr., of course. His strongest suits are an impressive control of the language and a quick wit. Jack Kemp is a type of opponent whom I find extremely difficult to debate: friendly, non-hostile, a "nice guy." If one tears into such a speaker, it creates sympathy for him/her in the audience. With Bill Buckley there are no complications since you can throw the kitchen sink at him while he is throwing the kitchen sink at you. Nice guys sometimes finish first. Max Schachtman, who died in 1972, was an old Communist-Trotskyist who wound up as a moderate social democrat who supported the war in Vietnam. In all of those political incarnations he remained a representative of a dying breed: passionate, dialectical, informed, Talmudic, and yet often quite funny. When debating Earl Browder, the former head of the American Communist Party who had been expelled in the forties, Schachtman conjured up the names of all the Communist leaders in Eastern Europe who had not only been deposed but executed. He then pointed at Browder and said, "There, but for the accident of geography, stands a corpse."

2. I think that a thorough knowledge of the subject *plus* an informed awareness of your opponent's strongest and most effective arguments is key. A good debater should be able to present the case against himself/herself as effectively as the person on the other side.

3. I don't think a killer instinct is necessary. Indeed, I think a debater who sees the contest as a means for the clarification of truth will, for that reason, be more effective. I don't say that this attitude should be adopted in order to be more effective. I merely note that it helps.

4. I believe that speaking last is an advantage for me. But then, I also think, rightly or wrongly, that I have a certain talent for summary and synthesis. On this point, as on any other, a speaker's sense of his/her strengths and weaknesses is critical.

5. Admit the mistake quickly and openly.

6. I would like to say that rhetorical devices are not important. Unfortunately they are. Indeed, I sometimes think that the timbre of a speaker's voice is (unfairly) a significant factor, too. Speaking—if

I may criticize a calling I have followed all my life—is a much less serious activity than writing, and listening is much less instructive than reading. I have never known an audience that can grasp more than three ideas.

7. In my experience—say, when I debated a representative of Chase Manhattan on tax policy and capital formation—representatives of large organizations are doing a job and often go by the numbers.

8. Inexperienced debaters (a) try to say too much; (b) try to kill their opponents when they have scored a point and thus either evoke sympathy for him/her or provoke him/her into an effective reply; (c) rely on mere rhetoric, which hardly ever works.

9. The most important thing with a hostile audience is not to let them get inside your head and change your arguments out of fear. Insults and stupid heckling are best ignored (with a microphone and an authoritative voice, that is easy enough), but a quick response to a heckler can sometimes be worth a whole speech.

10. Debating bothers me. To the degree that it can promote sophistry, I think it can corrupt personal life. My ideal is discussion, exchange, the mutual exploration of truth, not a polite war.

Howard Miller:

1. William Rusher, William F. Buckley, and Howard Jarvis. Rusher is the consummate intelligence as an arguer. He is especially powerful because of thorough preparation, eloquent precision in the use of language and the true destroyer's instinct for any weakness in an opponent's case. Buckley is especially difficult to debate because his style sets up a series of defense perimeters before an adversary can ever reach the substance. First one must get through humor, scorn, irony, sarcasm, invective, and finally, and hopefully, deal with the substance of the argument. Jarvis in his late 70s is the perfect combination of person, issue, and time. He is a classic example of exceptional circumstance overriding all the regular rules. He is feisty, abusive, rude, and devastating because his combination of age and energy stamp his sincerity, and the emotional impact of his issue guarantees attention.

2. Aside from the "spectacular" debate, such as with Howard Jarvis on tax reform, the single most important factor is attention to the facts. In the end, facts win arguments. Not eloquence, not wit, not passion, but only the facts. Eloquence, wit, and passion are frosting. Only a solid presentation of fact will carry the day. But what is a fact? It is extremely important for an arguer to understand the force and position of an opponent. No matter what side you take in an argument you may always be wrong, and a sense of certainty is the true Achilles' heel of most arguers. Even though you may think you disagree, if a position is held and believed by some significant number of people, then it has a human basis and deserves to be respected enough to be closely examined. You can't really defeat an argument unless you understand it, as opposed to dismissing it, and develop and present the facts that oppose it. All this means that you must really understand why you believe in your position. That is not as simple a matter as it seems, since all too many people adopt positions, and even agree to argue them, based on little more than faith, convenience, and background. That is not enough. Even the most deeply held beliefs must be subject to the strongest analysis before one should risk a public debate on them.

3. Yes. But not only a "killer instinct." The arguer must at the same time have both commitment, to the point of a "killer instinct," and objectivity to the point of being able to make a ruthless judgment on one's own effectiveness. It is the capacity to be simultaneously a participant and observer that distinguishes the truly great public arguer.

4. There are clearly some advantages to both, but on balance I would prefer to speak first. The person who speaks first, if that position is skillfully used, has the capacity to assume the offensive by establishing the issues, vocabulary, and concepts of the discussion. If the person responding answers on the terms set by the first speaker, then the debate is virtually over. The person speaking second must establish his own set of perceptions; do so in a way that does not appear discontinuous with what the first speaker has said; and then having done that, redefine the first speaker's statements in the light of the second speaker's terms. If the second speaker can do that, it will be a standoff and perhaps begin to shift the momentum. But

that is an extraordinary thing to do, and thus the first speaker normally has the continuous advantage throughout the debate.

5. Admit it. Gracefully if possible, awkwardly if necessary, but in any case admit it. The unwillingness to admit a mistake is one of the great weaknesses of many arguers. The consequence of not admitting when one has made a mistake is to destroy one of the most essential elements of the discussion: the speaker's credibility with the audience. On the other hand, the candid admission of an error, far from further damaging the speaker beyond what damage the mistake has already caused, will establish the speaker's credibility on all other points. In effect, the audience may think that since the arguer is being honest when there is a mistake he must be honest in the other assertions that are being made as well. The human nature of the speaker makes the candid admission of error one of the most difficult things to do, but the human nature of the audience makes it one of the most necessary and effective things to do.

6. Rhetorical devices can play a significant role in winning an argument when the underlying foundation and logic are secure. The risk is that if the rhetorical devices are not built on that solid foundation, they not only will be of no help but harm the debater by conveying an impression of style without substance.

7. The most important things are to speak to items that are within the common perception of the audience and to rely on a few but solidly established facts. The more complex you permit the argument to become, the more difficult it is for one arguing against a bureaucracy.

8. The commonest mistake is not to appreciate the weaknesses in one's argument. Anything worth debating publicly will normally have at least two credible sides. The inexperienced arguer seems to assume absolute correctness and so be exposed only during the debate to the strong points of the opponent and not to have thought through beforehand ways to deal with those strong points. In order to understand an opponent's strong points, the arguer must thoroughly prepare and focus on the facts of a position. One's own position with all its weakness must be completely understood.

9. In many ways a hostile audience is the easiest of audiences to handle. Before a hostile audience the arguer is in a no-lose situation.

Any convert is a net gain and perhaps unexpected. In addition, the dynamics of hostility from an audience may provide an unexpected opportunity. For example, a frequent mistake made by questioners from a hostile audience is to reveal overt audience reaction to the arguer. At that point, the arguer can emphasize his position as a guest of the audience. That tactic will not only still the rudeness but because of the unfair behavior sometimes make members of the audience more receptive to the debater's points. In short, as a matter of debate, one should never hesitate to go before a hostile audience, though, of course, if we were talking about political consequences outside the debate effect itself, there might be a whole different range of considerations.

10. Yes. It is especially important in teaching that one must have empathy with those on the other side and objectivity about oneself in order to function well in a wide variety of situations. And besides, it's fun.

Daniel Patrick Moynihan:

1. McGeorge Bundy, Robert McNamara, Henry Kissinger. Bundy is unrivaled at developing the logic of a position, especially in making your own end up seeming absurd. McNamara was master of data, much of it mistaken, but none of it refutable. Kissinger won his arguments by making you see that it was in your interest to lose to him.

2. Persistence. Quite seriously. Both in the political and academic worlds a position must be stated over and over and over until the advocate is bone weary of the subject. With luck, just before giving up entirely, some little sign of recognition will appear, and with it new resolve. I published my first article on the monstrous injustice of the Supreme Court rulings on aid to parochial schools in 1961. Last summer a Circuit Court judge in Pittsburgh repeated some of them. It only took eighteen years.

3. Don't know what a killer instinct is. I have the impression that a person who seems too aggressive loses audiences. Wm. F. Buckley, Jr.'s great strength as an arguer is his sometimes maddeningly unreasonable reasonableness.

4. Don't have enough experience to be sure. In the Senate I try to speak toward the end of the debate. But most important is to speak when someone is listening.

5. I don't know about an arguer, but a person of any integrity acknowledges the mistake right off.

6. Arguments are won by persuading others that their interests lie with your position. To win arguments you must learn to divine the interests of others—as they see them. MacBundy would often point out that large organizations rarely know what their best interests are. He was thinking especially of business. This obviously presents a dilemma to the candid controversialist.

7. Same as above. Make the organization think its interests—as it sees them—are compatible with your position.

8. Probably the commonest mistake, I am sorry to say, is being reasonable. Politics, as Mr. Dooley said, "ain't beanbag." It is much more like bear baiting. Academia is worse.

9. Be brief, acknowledge hostility, get out.

10. I really haven't argued formally a great deal save with my wife. Come to think of it, our twenty-fifth anniversary is not far off. May 29, I believe. She has usually prevailed through persistence.

Finally, here are the mini-essays of those who preferred to respond in that form:

Pat Buchanan:

An ability to argue—rather the perceived ability—allowed me to pass through six hours of nationally televised testimony before the Senate Watergate Committee—without having to cap my six-year career of White House service to Richard M. Nixon with a six-month compulsory vacation at Maxwell Air Force Base in Montgomery, Alabama.

From my own daily experience as a talk-show co-host and radio commentator on the NBC network "Confrontation," let me humbly offer the following counsel to that tiny few whose particular eccentricity is to purchase books written by William Rusher.

The purpose in an argument is not to win over one's adversary,

but to win over one's audience. An individual may emerge "victori-
ous" even if the audience has gone home unpersuaded.

The worst mistake an arguer can commit is to bore the assemblage
to distraction. The packaging and delivery system of the argument
are as important as the content. Surround each point with humor or
anecdote or historic analogy or uncommon quotation or the unfamil-
iar story. The audience is there not only to be informed, but entertained; it is as interested in the sherbet and pudding served up, as in
the meat and potatoes. Ergo, as much care should be devoted to the
preparation of the dessert as the preparation of the dinner.

The most common error of the amateur is to reveal, by expression,
that an antagonist's shaft has struck home—to exhibit that state of
agitated confusion known as "fluster."

While William F. Buckley, Jr., is the most impressive debater I
have witnessed in action, the most formidable—and frustrating—opponent to confront is the man with no heroes, the man who will defend no ideological terrain.

Lastly, when caught *in flagrante* by an opponent, one should concede nothing—but imitate a motorist flagged down by a foot patrol-
man for running a stop sign. Look directly ahead and stand up on
the accelerator. There is at least the chance you will not have to pay
the fine.

John Kenneth Galbraith:

The first rule for successful debating is, of course, to have the req-
uisite information. Liberals sometimes substitute righteousness for
information; conservatives normally substitute passion, indignation,
nostalgia, and deeply vacuous affirmations on the injustices being
suffered by the rich. If you are devoid of information, it may be good
personal strategy to decline the debate, unprecedented though such
action may be.

If you suspect your opponent of being devoid of information, press
him relentlessly and do not hesitate to be specific.

"You say, Mr. Rusher, that the oil companies are suffering from
deeply inadequate earnings? What were Mobil's profits as a percent-
age of sales last year? And what figure would you, sir, consider adequate?"

Next you must be prepared for the speaker who, by his very eloquence and stream-of-consciousness speech, monopolizes the discussion. Never try to interrupt. Let him finish and then ask him to repeat.

"That was an impressive statement, Professor Friedman. But I expect our listeners lost track, just as I did. Could you go back over it again?"

The same method works well for the debater who resorts, also at length, to a combination of assertion, repetition, parentheses, appeals to popular cupidity, public gullibility, and sadistically tortured logic. You cannot possibly correct him. So you say:

"I'm not sure I quite followed your argument, Professor Laffer. Would you explain more fully?"

The rule is the same in both cases. Never try to destroy an opponent if he can be counted upon to destroy himself. If his first marathon round doesn't totally repel the audience, you can be sure the reprise will.

When these speakers have exhausted their audience, you move in and—if you haven't developed the same habit as they—you clarify the position to your taste in a few well-considered and wholly grammatical sentences. Often you can imply that this is what your opponent was really trying to say. No one will ever know.

Next, when you are accused of something bad in a debate, unless it is illegal or insupportably immoral, admit to it immediately and, if possible, to something worse. That shows that the accusation was wholly unimportant.

"You are a closet socialist, I believe, Professor Galbraith."

"As to being a socialist, quite right, Mr. Simon. So many are these days, as you see them. But I like to think of myself as quite out in the open."

"You are a socialist, Professor Galbraith?"

"Right, Mr. Wriston. I mess around with health care and low-cost housing. But I'm not a very effective one. You and Mr. Rockefeller and the people at Manufacturers Hanover really do something for socialism when you tell a corporation that its only chance is to get down to Washington and see what the boys there can do."

"You always come out for more government regulation, Ken."

"Never so ardently as this morning, Bill. I just heard that you and Pat are going home by way of San Diego on a DC-10."

Finally all debaters should remember that debating is like football and not like football. Like football, it doesn't much matter next day who won. Unlike football, no one knows.

Phyllis Schlafly:

The most important single factor in winning an argument is to be specific and factual. Generalizations are losers. The more specific you can be in presenting the facts and the arguments that support your case, the more persuasive you are sure to be.

To be a good arguer, one does not have to have a "killer instinct." The objective is to persuade, not to kill. You persuade by making effective arguments, not by demolishing your opponent. The exception to this rule is television. A "killer instinct" often helps you to score when you only have thirty seconds to make a point.

The purely rhetorical devices (as distinguished from cogency and logic of argumentation) are unworthy of the serious debater, and should be left to the entertainer. Rhetorical devices from a bag of tricks may make an audience cheer or laugh, but they do not win an argument.

It doesn't really matter whether one speaks first or last in debate so long as two rules of fairness are respected: There must be time allowed to each side for rebuttal, and the one who speaks last must be forbidden to present new arguments that the other side has no chance to refute. If those conditions are not present, it is better to speak last.

The most common mistake made by an inexperienced arguer is to let his emotions overtake his objectivity. When you lose your temper, you also lose the argument. If you cannot argue a question without becoming emotionally involved, don't argue in public—you can't win. There are at least two sides to nearly every argument, and opponents should be able to disagree without being disagreeable.

The most difficult opponent to deal with in debate is one who unfairly steals more than her fair share of the time (sometimes called diarrhea of the mouth). It is difficult to win an argument if you have

20 percent of the time to your opponent's 80 percent, and when your skill and energies must be devoted to trying to get a word in edgewise. It eases the strain on everybody (including the onlookers) if you first establish fair time rules.

The second most difficult opponent to deal with is the one who confidently (or arrogantly) tells untruths. The only way to cope with this is to respond with specifics rather than generalities.

The least difficult opponent to deal with is the one who indulges in the *ad hominem* (or *ad mulierem*) personal attack. That shoddy tactic is a loser before any audience. Just tell your listeners that the attack reminds you of the lesson the old lawyer gave the young lawyer: "If you are weak on the law, argue the facts. If you are weak on the facts, argue the law. If you are weak on both the law and the facts, abuse your opponent."

Coping with the personal attack, as well as facing a hostile audience, requires, first of all, that you keep your cool. Secondly, don't try to return tit for tat or answer with a smart-alecky retort. Don't try to put down or attack those who disagree with you. Just keep presenting your argument, calmly, objectively, and factually. You can win your audience's respect even if you don't persuade them to accept your point of view.

It's too bad that so much real-life arguing is spoiled when your opponent becomes uptight and upset, or tries to upstage you with semantic or theatrical tricks, or unnerves the audience by making personal attacks. Arguing, when done with good faith, good reason, good temper, and good humor is the most stimulating of all competitions.

David Schoenbrun:

There are a couple of basic "do's and don'ts" for a successful debater but the essential element, the absolute necessity, is to believe passionately in your own argument. There must be total commitment to the wisdom and righteousness of your own cause. There is no middle ground, no on-the-other-hand. There is only right and wrong, and you are right and your opponent is wrong. Doubt is destructive, tolerance is weakness in a debate.

There is a danger inherent in this stand: the danger of treating your opponent as not only wrong-minded but possibly sinister, evil, unpatriotic. That is the very first and most important "don't." Do not indulge in *ad hominem* attacks on the adversary, much as you may loathe him and his arguments. Most audiences enjoy a good fight, even a fiery clash between opponents, but, as in a prize fight— and debates *are* fights—audiences will turn quickly against anyone who strikes a low blow.

Ridicule an opponent's arguments, poke genial fun at him, twit him, tease him, be witty, but DO NOT be cruel and mean. DO NOT smear an opponent, no McCarthyism, no direct or even sly charges of Communism, no suggestions of any kind that your opponent is anything but an honest, loyal American, unless, of course, the sonuvabitch really isn't honest, decent, and loyal, in which case you should not agree to be on a platform with him or her.

Next to true belief, the fundamental of the successful debater is mastery of the subject. Do your homework. Be FULLY prepared. You can demolish an opponent if you catch him in an error of fact or clearly faulty reasoning in which vital elements of the case in point are left out. Sometimes an opponent may overlook a salient point. Catch him out and hint that the oversight was deliberate. A useful phrase is: Why didn't you tell these good people that . . .

DO NOT make any assumptions about your audience and do not try to be tricky by playing up to or buttering up your audience. Outside of the Communist Party and the John Birch Society it is difficult to know just what your audience is thinking. Concentrate on your own deeply held convictions and make your own best case. You can get through to an audience even if on the surface it might seem to be stacked against you. Self-confidence, conviction, enthusiasm are infectious so long as you stay below the line of arrogance.

Be clear, be lucid, avoid complicated expositions and esoteric language. Bill Buckley's esoteric vocabulary impresses the readers of his columns and books, but it is not a good tool of debate. In a debate on Vietnam in Phoenix, I scored points on Buckley on this very issue. He talked, for example, of a "placebo" and told the audience not to swallow it. In my turn, I asked him why he didn't just simply speak English and warn them against a certain argument being a phony sugar pill. "These are good and intelligent people here; just tell them in good old American what you are talking about. We don't need highfalutin Yale Latin here." Bill was furious with me and accused me later of "playing up to the audience." I laughed and answered: "You're damn right. It's better to talk up to them than down to them, particularly when I was being brought into Phoenix to debate you, in front of Peggy Goldwater and Claire Booth Luce, like Daniel in the lion's den." Buckley is a formidable debater but he does sometimes shoot too high above the audience. You can get away with that if you are the sole speaker, and you can dazzle your audience, as Buckley can, but beware of trying that in a debate.

Be careful how you attack your opponent. Do not make your audience uncomfortable. Use wit, not sarcasm. Use a rapier, not a club. And when you stab your opponent, keep smiling and let it be known that it is all in good fun and part of the debating game. But DO NOT play games about your main arguments.

Speak clearly in a strong, firm, but modulated voice. DO NOT shout, do not yell. Vary the rhythms and tones of your voice and delivery. Sometimes drop the volume of your voice and make them strain just a bit to hear you, then come up in volume to drive home your point.

If your opponent scores a strong point on you or gets in a witty stab, smile, laugh, and join the crowd in generous applause. You might be a good sport and so confident of the justice and wisdom of your own case, that you can take everything the other side throws at you in the best of spirits.

Finally, try to be precise and do not take extra time or words. DO NOT be windy. If you are given five minutes for an opening statement, take four and a half. Try to avoid forcing the referee to gavel you down. Always be cheerful and pleasant at the end. Shake hands, throw your arms around the shoulders of your opponent, and be the first to do it.

INDEX

evidence and, 78 ff.; marshaling the facts and, 78–108; predicting the consequences and, 105–8; questioning, 84 ff., 109 ff., 168–73; rhetorical devices and, 110 ff.; sizing up the opposition and, 61–65; use of analogies and, 102–5 ff.
Eye contact, 119–20

"Face Off" debates ("Good Morning, America" program), viii, 9
Facts (factual data, evidence, information), 20 ff.; advice by experts and, 188, 192–93, 194, 196; arguing for clarification of, 10–13; arguing with politicians and, 162–73; attacking opponent's, 92–101; basic structure of arguments and, 20–24; countering, 66–67; defined, 66–67; defining the issues and, 10–13, 25–37; establishing, 78–92; expert evidence and, 78–92 ff.; planted axiom and, 72–74; predicting consequences and, 105–8; relevance and irrelevance and, 97 ff.; rhetorical devices and, 110 ff.; successful arguing and, 20–24; techniques of argumentation and marshaling of, 66 ff., 78–108; unknown, ethics and revealing to the opposition, 63–65; use of analogies and, 102–5 ff.
Family (personal) arguments, 133, 134–36
Farber, Barry, 59, 60
Farber, M. A., 87
Faulk, John Henry, 119
Fighting (see also Aggressions): arguing as alternative to, 2
Firemen, right to strike by, 89–92
First Amendment, 72
Fonda, Jane, 160
Fontanne, Lynn, 2
Forced busing issue, 33, 84
Ford, Gerald R., 128–30
Formal organized arguments, 134, 154–56. See also specific aspects, kinds
Frankel, Max, 128–29

Galbraith, John Kenneth, 61, 156–57, 183; advice by, 192–94
Gallacher, William (Willie), 131–32
Gamesmanship, 126
Germany. See Nazi Germany

Gofman, John, 180–81
Going first or second. See Speaking first or last
Goldwater, Barry, 42
Goldwater, Peggy, 197
Goodman, Allan, 112–13
"Good Morning, America" program, "Face Off" debates on, viii, 9
Government, arguments with, 133, 134, 142, 145–50, 184, 185, 187, 189. See also specific agencies, bodies
Gray (Gordon) Board, 99–101
Great Britain (England, the British), 28, 115, 123, 131–32, 147, 154, 175, 178 (see also specific individuals); and World War II intervention issue, 67–72

Harrington, Michael, 183, 184; advice by, 186–87
Hartnett, Vincent, 119
Hatch, Orrin, 47
Hatfield, Mark, 93
Hauptmann, Bruno, 122
Hazelton, Nika, 141
Heckling, coping with hostile audiences and, 174–75, 187
Heilbroner, Robert, 48–50
Heller, Walter, 61
Helsinki Agreement, 128
Hiroshima, Japan, 81
Hiss, Alger, 117
Hitler, Adolf, 67, 68, 123, 132
Ho Chi Minh, 160
Hook, Sidney, 184
Hostile audiences, coping with, 174–75, 184, 185, 187, 189–90, 191, 195
House of Representatives, U. S., 134, 146–50. See also Congress, U. S.
Housman, A. E., 126
Hughes, Howard, 85
Humor. See Wit
Hunter College (N.Y.C.) debates, 166–67
Husband vs. wife arguments, 133, 134–36

Immigration Service, U. S., 146–47
Incredulity, 109, 119, 180
Indifference, conveying of, 120
Informal organized arguments, 134, 151–54, 156–73. See also specific aspects, kinds

William Rusher is a national personality—he lectures widely, is a television commentator, a syndicated columnist, publisher of *National Review*, and, as of January 5, 1981, broadcasts three commentaries per week for Westinghouse Radio's Group W network. Above all, he is recognized as one of the country's leading debaters. For four years, he pleaded, proved, refuted, and rebutted as one of PBS's "The Advocates," and was seen regularly on the "Face Off" mini-debate segment of ABC Television's "Good Morning, America." Mr. Rusher lives in New York City.